BUILDING A SUSTAINABLE INTERNATIONAL ORDER
A RAND Project to Explore U.S. Strategy in a Changing World

TESTING THE VALUE OF THE
Postwar International Order

Michael J. Mazarr
Ashley L. Rhoades

T0302942

Prepared for the Office of Net Assessment, Office of the Secretary of Defense
Approved for public release; distribution unlimited

For more information on this publication, visit www.rand.org/t/RR2226

Library of Congress Cataloging-in-Publication Data is available for this publication.
ISBN: 978-0-8330-9977-8

Published by the RAND Corporation, Santa Monica, Calif.
© Copyright 2018 RAND Corporation
RAND® is a registered trademark.

Support RAND
Make a tax-deductible charitable contribution at
www.rand.org/giving/contribute

www.rand.org

Preface

This project was sponsored by the Office of Net Assessment, Office of the Secretary of Defense, and conducted within the International Security and Defense Policy Center of the RAND National Defense Research Institute, a federally funded research and development center sponsored by the Office of the Secretary of Defense, the Joint Staff, the Unified Combatant Commands, the Navy, the Marine Corps, the defense agencies, and the defense Intelligence Community. For more information on the RAND International Security and Defense Policy Center, see rand.org/nsrd/ndri/centers/isdp or contact the director (contact information is provided on the web page).

Contents

Figures and Tables

Summary

Since 1945, the United States has pursued its interests in part through the creation and maintenance of international economic institutions, global organizations including the United Nations and G-7, bilateral and regional security organizations including alliances, and liberal political norms that collectively are often referred to as the "international order." In recent years, rising powers have begun to challenge aspects of this order. This report is based on a RAND project, entitled "Building a Sustainable International Order," that aims to understand the existing order, assess its status and current challenges, and recommend future U.S. policies.

The study has produced multiple reports and essays.[1] Other analyses in the study have defined the order, assessed its current status, and pointed to alternative structures for future world orders, as well as evaluating the approaches of specific countries to the order. The purpose of this report is very specific: to evaluate the order's value—to assess its role in promoting U.S. goals and interests, as well as shared global objectives.[2] To answer the question of the order's value, we first

---

[1]   These are available at the project website:
www.rand.org/nsrd/projects/international-order/publications

[2]   The authors acknowledge the strong support of Seth Jones, director of the International Security and Defense Policy Center of the RAND National Security Research Division, during the course of this project. We are also grateful to the sponsor, the Office of Net Assessment, U.S. Department of Defense, for making the research possible. And we appreciate the helpful comments of James Dobbins and Charles Glaser, our peer reviewers, as well as the earlier, more informal comments provided by Lisa Martin and William Wohlforth. Full responsibility for the contents of this report lies with the authors.

had to define the components of the order that we proposed to evaluate for possible value to U.S. interests. We then reviewed broad assessments of the order, as well as detailed empirical work on its specific components.

Defining the Order

Many treatments of the postwar order focus on its primary institutions—the United Nations, the General Agreement on Tariffs and Trade and World Trade Organization system, the U.S. alliance structure, the World Bank and International Monetary Fund, the G-7 and G-20, and the hundreds of subsidiary organizations, treaties, and conventions of the institutional order. Those elements embody a critical component of the postwar order, but we find that two other elements must be included to understand its true importance. One is the level of identifiable multilateral collaboration that has come to characterize many state interactions in a globalizing era. The other is the emergence of an implicit community of largely like-minded, order-producing states at the core of world politics. Taken together, these three components—the institutional order, the demonstrated propensity toward multilateral action, and the core group of states—compose what we mean in this report by the *postwar order*.

Measuring the Order's Effects—and Value

Evaluating the effects of the postwar order is a challenging task. Many factors conspire to produce the results sought by the order—global economic growth, peace and stability, democratization—and it can be difficult to separate out the effect of specific institutions or actions. Scholars have tried to do so with regard to particular elements of the order, such as human rights treaties and environmental agreements, but many of these studies are either highly conditional or disputed by other studies, or else they simply end up highlighting the role of many independent factors in generating outcomes.

As a result, our research in fact suggests that the components of the postwar order can *only* have significant effects when pooled with other factors, ranging from U.S. power to supportive international opinion to associated macroeconomic trends. Our approach therefore emphasizes the *complementarity among variables* rather than the unique effect of specific factors.

The question then is whether the role of the order has been important at all—whether it is simply window dressing on outcomes that would have emerged in any case. To answer that question, we reviewed multiple sources of evidence. The foundation of the research was a review of hundreds of studies assessing the effects of specific components of the order, such as trade treaties or human rights conventions. We used data and trends gathered in earlier studies to make our own assessments of causal links between elements of the order and key U.S. goals. Our earlier work on the relationship of key countries to the order provided information on the public statements and private views of major countries. And we continued to conduct background dialogues to elicit expert judgment from U.S. officials who have attempted to promote U.S. interests in the context of the overarching order, gathering evidence from people who have worked at the intersection of the order and U.S. policy to assess whether the two are complementary. The resulting analysis produced five major findings.

Finding 1: The Postwar Order Offers Significant Value to U.S. Interests and Objectives

A combination of quantitative evidence, case studies, and expert validation suggests that the postwar order has had important value in legitimizing and strengthening U.S. influence and institutionalizing and accelerating positive trends. This report surveys three specific issue areas: economic affairs, security affairs, and norms and values. Within these three areas, the report identifies 14 categories of value, outlined in Table S.1. In each case it cites quantitative and case-based evidence for the causal relationship between elements of the order and positive outcomes.

Table S.1
Categories of Evaluation

Postwar International Order: Categories of Value Assessed

Security Affairs

- The norms and preferences of the core group of states change the risk calculus for potential aggressors
- Military alliances deter regional conflict
- Conflict resolution institutions help avoid or end conflicts
- Peacekeeping activities share the burden of global peace enforcement
- Nonproliferation institutions and norms constrain weapons of mass destruction

Economic Affairs

- Lowered trade barriers from global, regional, and bilateral treaties
- Interaction with domestic interest groups to promote liberal economic values
- Institutional and normative engines of effective response to economic crises
- Efficiency and innovation gains through standards, agreements, and networks
- Material and nonmaterial attraction of the predominant economic core

Norms and Values

- Norms, institutions, and expectations of the order promote the rule of law
- Norms and institutions constrain international criminal activities
- Advancing transparency and anticorruption initiatives
- Promoting human rights through the normative context created by conventions and treaties

The order has such value for the United States in part because its outcomes strongly support the goals and processes of the U.S. grand strategy. When considering the benefits of the postwar order, the whole is in fact greater than the sum of the parts: the collective effect of the order has limited but important influence over the preferences and behavior of states. Examples that can be verified with case-study or empirical evidence include the influence of the order's multilateral sensibility, both within alliances and more broadly; the gravitational effect of an integrated global market and the conditions for membership of its leading institutions; and the role of long-term normative socialization. Taken together—and again, combined with the role of other factors, such as U.S. power and global trends—the postwar order has created a form of dynamic equilibrium in the international system that has promoted stability and reduced uncertainty.

Finding 2: Specifically in Quantifiable and Return-on-Investment Terms, the Order Contributes to Outcomes with Measurable Value and Appears to Have a Strongly Positive Cost-Benefit Calculus

Beyond the qualitative factors referenced in the first finding, we also evaluated the possible quantitative, measurable value of the order. We assessed ten illustrative issues and located the best estimates available for their economic value—whether avoiding protectionism, securing allied support for conflicts, or controlling piracy. In each case we offered a judgment, based on historical comparisons, of a potential counterfactual scenario absent the existence of the order in order to help understand the causal relationships.

As with all estimates of the order's value, it is difficult to distinguish variables associated with the order from other factors. We have assessed cases in which it is possible that the order, while not the sole variable, is responsible for some proportion of the value. The result is necessarily suggestive and cannot be precise, but the sum total of value is significant. In each of these examples, we find specific causal evidence that the elements of the order were either a necessary condition or a strongly contributing variable to realizing this value. To the extent that the institutions, relationships, norms, and implicit communities of the order have played a necessary role in avoiding even *one* of these major negative outcomes, the value dwarfs the investments the United States makes in the order.

Finding 3: The Postwar Order Represents a Leading U.S. Competitive Advantage

The U.S.-led order has served as an important source of U.S. competitive advantage in the postwar world. This is not to suggest that the order has disproportionately benefited the United States as opposed to others, though some empirical work suggests that this may indeed be true in several narrow issue areas, such as the degree of influence in international organizations. More broadly, though, it could be argued that the order has benefited others more than America. It has, for example, created a context in which some states have experienced faster and longer-lasting economic growth than the United States. As a result, relative U.S. predominance has gradually declined. It has committed the United States to bearing a disproportionate share of the global burden of security, allowing other states to enhance investments in nondefense areas.

But the postwar order—and the associated U.S. grand strategy—was never designed to keep relative advantage over friends and partners. It aimed to nurture multiple reservoirs of stability and values in the international system beyond the United States as a way of creating a context in which U.S. interests would be safer. The competitive advantage provided by the postwar order thus comes not in terms of relative advantage *over* others but rather in the support it has provided to the overall U.S. grand strategy. It has created a context in which others would be more likely to support U.S. efforts than they would otherwise have been. As the leader and sponsor of a multilateral order, the United States has not been merely another great power: It has been the architect of a system of mutual advantage. This simple fact has carried significant geopolitical advantage.

Specific institutions have worked alongside U.S. diplomacy to achieve U.S. objectives. Alliances and partnerships have fueled burden sharing. Norms promulgated by the order provide reference points to hold states accountable to progress in specific directions. The result has been a safer, more stable, and more prosperous world, which has translated into a smaller burden for U.S. national security policy.

By providing a vision of a better world, one shaped by the United States and reflecting its values but representing an aspiration for the world community, the postwar order has also lashed U.S. power to a broadly endorsed purpose. This legitimizing function has had benefits for the United States. Most notably, it has meant that few if any states have perceived a need to undertake classic balancing of American power—thus potentially saving the United States tens of billions of dollars in additional defense expenditures that would have been necessary had others sought to balance its power more aggressively.

Finding 4: If the United States Wants to Continue to Lead Globally, Some Form of Order Is Vital

If the United States were to adopt a radically different global posture—for example, a form of retrenchment—the cost-benefit equation of a shared order might change. Even in that case, some components of the order—such as a multilateral economic system—would remain useful in protecting U.S. vital interests. But an important finding of this analysis is that *if* the United States wants to continue to lead globally, a functioning international order is indispensable. Without the benefits and legitimacy conferred by such an order, vibrant U.S. leadership would likely become financially and strategically unaffordable.

Finding 5: A Functioning Multilateral Order Will Be Essential to Deal with Emerging Security and Economic Issues

The report looks ahead to the security and economic issues likely to dominate the U.S. agenda in coming years, including managing stable strategic competitions, dealing with climate change, building a more just economy, and engaging in counterterrorism. It concludes that the United States would have greater difficulty in addressing the risks to its security and prosperity in such issues outside the context of an effective multilateral order. More broadly, we find that at a time of growing rivalry, nationalism, and uncertainty, a functioning multilateral order will be essential to provide stabilizing ballast to an increasingly unruly global environment.

Conclusion

These findings represent a qualified but still powerful endorsement of the essential American conception of its role in the world. Support for a form of world order, both as an instrumental tool to safeguard American interests and as a collective effort to shape a better future, is part of the American ethos. While the form of the U.S. global role has evolved, these principles have reflected a particularly American expression of international interests. That the postwar variety of this endeavor has measurably contributed to those interests reemphasizes the continuing relevance of this quintessentially American vision.

CHAPTER ONE

Introduction

Skeptics of multilateralism and international institutions, in both politics and academia, have raised fresh doubts about the value of the postwar international order for U.S. national interests. Whether in terms of the global set of alliances, the United Nations system, the postwar trade architecture, or arms control and climate agreements, critics are calling into question what the United States has gained from its international engagement and the set of institutions, treaties, and conventions it has helped establish since 1945. These doubts are interwoven with a new populist sensibility that is skeptical of international norms, agreements, and institutions.

This study is one part of a larger RAND project, entitled "Building a Sustainable International Order," which aims to understand the existing order, assess its status and current challenges, and recommend future U.S. policies. Other analyses in the study have defined the order, assessed its current status, and pointed to alternative structures for future world orders, as well as evaluating the approaches of specific countries to the order. The purpose of this report is very specific: to evaluate the order's value—to assess its role in promoting U.S. goals and interests, as well as shared global objectives. To answer the question of the order's value, we first had to define the components of the order that we proposed to evaluate for possible value to U.S. interests. We then reviewed broad assessments of the order, as well as detailed empirical work on its specific components. Because of the wide range of issues to be examined, and the availability of existing empirical research, this analysis represents a survey of existing research rather than an effort to generate new data in a few narrow areas. It also benefits from discussions, as part of the larger project, with current and former U.S. officials and representatives of international organizations.

In one sense, given the broad record of the last 70 years, the case for the postwar order's value seems obvious. It has coincided with the acceleration of global trends of hugely positive value for U.S. and shared global interests: the explosion of an unprecedented degree of prosperity; the emergence of a period of great-power peace and the continued decline of interstate conflict as a tool for resolving disputes; the emergence of dozens of major and minor forums through which states have coordinated joint responses to collective security issues; and the continued growth (until the last few years) of the level of global democracy, as well as what has been termed a global "human rights revolution." Many sources we consulted, and former officials with whom we spoke, agreed on a basic, overarching theme: It is very difficult to imagine the impressive postwar trajectory of growth, democratization, and relative stability without the supporting architecture of an institutionalized multilateral order. Figure 1.1 highlights the broad correlations between postwar positive trends and the ways in which a multilateral order has helped to bring them about.

Yet the relationship between these outcomes and the order could be nothing more than coincidence. Other factors could be solely responsible for these historic achievements: U.S. power has guaranteed the peace in key regions, while globalization and productivity gains have been responsible for economic advances. Institutions, some believe, embody states' self-declared interests and assist states in achieving them. They do not change the conception of those interests.[1]

Attempting to evaluate the value of the postwar international order is a complex undertaking, because that order contains too many different components to be measured in simple terms. Answering the question demands that we assess military alliances, multilateral treaties and conventions, international organizations (both formal and informal), the effectiveness of specific rules associated with that whole archi-

---

[1]   Von Stein, 2005.

Figure 1.1
The Postwar Order and Leading Positive Trends

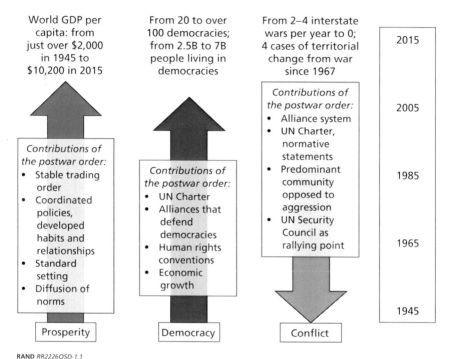

RAND RR2226OSD-1.1

tecture, and the effect of sometimes unwritten norms in shaping state behavior. No single indicator, or small set of them, will provide an unequivocal measurement.

Based on a review of the complex evidence that is available, our research suggests that the postwar order has made significant contributions—in particular by *reinforcing* other factors, such as U.S. power and macroeconomic trends—in achieving U.S. goals. This analysis points not to the independent causal value of the order but rather to how well it has achieved specified goals *in combination with* other instruments of statecraft.

This assessment of the value of the postwar order relates its benefits to a specific U.S. grand strategy—the theory of deep global engagement that, in one form or another, has characterized U.S. strategy since 1945. If the United States were to adopt a radically different global posture—for example, a form of retrenchment—the cost-benefit equation might change. Even in that case, however, some components of the order—such as a multilateral economic system—would remain useful in protecting U.S. vital interests. But an important finding of this analysis is that *if* the United States wants to continue to lead globally on multiple issues and in multiple regions, a functioning international order plays a critical role in reducing the costs of that role and the potential reactions to it. Without the benefits and legitimacy conferred by such an order, vibrant U.S. leadership on anything like the current model would likely become financially and strategically unaffordable.

This is true in part because the U.S.-led postwar order has allowed the United States to retain a disproportionate effect in rule setting while fashioning a legitimate international order of institutions and rules that helped to stabilize world politics. The postwar order, in other words, allowed the United States to pursue two key goals—safeguarding U.S. interests and using international collaboration as a means of solving problems—in mutually complementary ways.[2] This pattern was evident on a wide variety of issues, from international trade policy to human rights conventions to nonproliferation.[3]

Our analysis also suggests that the multilateral order has served as an important—and perhaps the overriding—source of U.S. competitive advantage in the postwar world. Specific institutions have worked alongside U.S. diplomacy to achieve U.S. objectives. Alliances and partnerships have fueled burden sharing. Norms promulgated by the order provide reference points to hold states accountable to prog-

---

[2]   Ikenberry, 2001, 2011; Gilpin, 1983; Ruggie, 1993.

[3]   See, for example, Foot, MacFarlane, and Mastanduno, 2003. There is also reason to believe that the United States gains indirect influence through its role in such institutions. James Vreeland has offered some of the most compelling evidence that the UN Security Council provides "private benefits" to the permanent five members, especially the United States. Vreeland's work also suggests that influence transfers across institutions: Powerful states can use leverage from one international organization (the UN) to gain greater voice in another (such as the International Monetary Fund [IMF]). This networked influence can be achieved by secondary powers, but the United States has been the dominant practitioner of the strategy (Lim and Vreeland, 2013; Vreeland and Dreher, 2014).

ress in specific directions. The result has been a safer, more stable, and more prosperous world, which has translated into a smaller burden for U.S. national security policy. And by providing a vision of a better world, one shaped by the United States and reflecting its values but representing an aspiration for the world community, the postwar order has lashed U.S. power to a broadly endorsed purpose.

It is important to stress, however, that other work in this project makes clear that the balance between U.S. predominance and the order's legitimacy is changing.[4] An overly self-interested vision of an order will be counterproductive. The bargain struck in the West after 1945—to accept an American-dominated order in exchange for U.S. protection and the promise of shared economic markets and prosperity—is fraying, because many more states are demanding a larger voice in the operation of the order. The United States must increasingly share operation of the order to keep it legitimate.

But the essential connection at the heart of the order, the relationship between U.S. interests and a multilateral vision, remains highly relevant. Our findings constitute an endorsement of the essential American conception of its role in the world.[5] Support for a form of world order, both as an instrumental tool to safeguard American interests and as the hope for a better future, is part of the American ethos. While the form of the U.S. global role has evolved, these principles have reflected a particularly American expression of international interests since the founding of the republic. That the postwar variety of this endeavor has measurably contributed to those interests and that hope—alongside the necessary parallel contributions of U.S. power and predominance and positive global economic and political trends—points to the continuing relevance and importance of this quintessentially American vision.

---

[4] Mazarr, Cevallos, et al., 2017.

[5] Ruggie, 1994, pp. 554–555.

CHAPTER TWO

Defining the Postwar International Order

The concept of international order has various meanings. An order, we argued in an earlier report for this project, "is a stable, structured pattern of relationships among states that involves some combination of parts, ranging from emergent norms to rule-making institutions to international political organizations or regimes."[1] An order is differentiated from the more general concept of an international system by this settled, structured character. G. John Ikenberry similarly defines an order as a set of "governing arrangements between states, including its fundamental rules, principles, and institutions."[2]

This is not meant to imply that an order is unchanging—both orders and systems evolve over time. In a purely definitional sense, however, an order refers to organizing mechanisms or structures that can exist in a larger, international system that may be more or less chaotic, anarchic, or evolving. Given such understandings of the concept of order, we sought to compare the value of the postwar order not to complete anarchy but rather to a hypothetical postwar world with many of the same systemic features (a Cold War followed by a period of U.S. predominance, along with many other aspects of the system) but lacking the defining components of a structured order—institutions, norms, rules, and (as will be argued later) patterns of multilateral cooperation and an emergent international community of states committed to the norms of the order. We are measuring the value of

---

[1] Mazarr, Priebe, et al., 2016, p. 7.

[2] Ikenberry, 2001, p. 23.

the order, in other words, against an alternative case of a similar world without that order.

In the narrowest sense, then, in this report we are concerned with the effects on state behavior and long-term outcomes in international relations of the specific normative and institutional elements of the current pattern of relationships—what might be called the "institutional order." The institutional order includes such elements as the baseline of international organizations—including the United Nations system and U.S. alliances—that provide forums for collective dialogue and action and for managing key issues such as financial stability; the large set of multilateral treaties, agreements, and conventions establishing rules of the road on issues ranging from trade to human rights; and networks of informal organizations and networks. In a longer-term sense, it also incorporates the socialization effects and norms of behavior that arise in connection with the emergence of the first three elements of the institutional order.

This study sought to evaluate the ways these institutions, and associated rule sets and emergent norms, have affected the preferences and behavior of states. At the same time, the full character of the postwar order reflects two aspects beyond a list of its major institutions. First, it embodies the broader principle of multilateralism that has long characterized the U.S. vision of world politics. As John Gerard Ruggie has defined it, a multilateral order "embodies rules of conduct that are commonly applicable to all countries," rather than discriminatory ones. It recognizes shared interests among states and offers mechanisms for "joint action." It reflects some degree of collective security, as well as "a commitment to national self-determination and universal human rights."[3] The value of the order lies in part in the potential significance of this larger vision, and the degree to which actual events have achieved part of its promise.

Another characteristic of the postwar order beyond its list of institutions, rules, and norms lies in the core group of like-minded states, a group whose interests converge sufficiently on a number of issues for it to reflect a critical mass of power and purpose in the interna-

---

[3]   Ruggie, 1994, pp. 556–557.

tional sphere. The institutional order has become the connective tissue for a group of largely like-minded states, built around the core set of value-sharing democracies.[4] This group has gradually come to reflect an embryonic and incomplete form of international community, whose basic preferences converge on several major points, such as a belief in the risks and costs of aggressive or selfish action. The result has been the emergence of a critical mass of countries that create a gravitational pull with disproportionate global influence. When combined with conditions for joining the core group, this situation can affect preferences and behavior.[5] This analysis does not make the case that this informal coalition at the heart of the order will survive, only that its influence has helped to produce the outcomes of the postwar order. Other studies in the project contend that sustaining the effect of this gravitational core should be a primary focus of U.S. strategy.

When we seek to measure the value of the postwar order, therefore, we are looking to the combined effects of three components of that order:

- its specific institutions, rules, and norms (the institutional order)
- the ways in which the principle and practice of multilateralism shape world politics
- the attractive and sometimes coercive influence of the predominant collection of value-sharing states that represent the core membership of the order.

The true effects of any international order can only be understood by considering this fusion of components—the institutional order, the principles of state conduct it reflects, and the combined preferences of the community of states that compose its membership. These three elements taken together are what should be understood as the prevailing global order.

---

[4] See Mazarr, 2017.

[5] Snyder, 2013a, p. 219.

CHAPTER THREE

Measuring the Influence of the Order

Any analyst hoping to assess the value of the postwar order immediately confronts a methodological problem. In an environment as complex as international politics, how can we hope to separate out the effect of specific institutions or actions? Scholars have tried to do so with regard to particular elements of the order, such as human rights treaties, using both regression analyses, which aim to distinguish among variables, and case research, which tries to discover the unique basis for specific actions in particular cases. But many of these studies are either highly conditional or disputed by other studies, or else they simply highlight the role of many independent factors in generating outcomes. Measuring the ways the order has effects beyond the sum of its parts is especially difficult.

We do not argue that the order's elements have had independent, binding effects on the behavior of states. Indeed, our research suggests that the components of the institutional order can *only* have significant effects when pooled with other factors, ranging from U.S. power to supportive international opinion to associated macroeconomic trends.[1]

---

[1] This approach has much in common with the "defensive realist" conception of the role of institutions and multilateralism—or, as Charles Glaser has phrased it, "contingent realism." The concept holds that institutions emerge to reflect, not control, state preferences—but that cooperation can be an effective form of self-help, and the elements of a multilateral order can flourish to the degree state interests allow. A key question is *under what conditions* self-help would generate cooperation—a question, our analysis would suggest, that the multilateral order can help influence. Our approach does place more emphasis on the potential value of institutions as catalysts to help realize the value of latent cooperative possibilities. See, for example, Glaser, 1994–1995, esp. pp. 57–60, 81–85; and Glaser, 2010.

The question then is whether, given those other factors, the role of the institutional order has been important at all—whether it is simply window dressing on outcomes that would have emerged in any case.[2]

The array of empirical and case-study research consulted for this analysis points to at least three major factors helping to shape postwar outcomes, reflected in Figure 3.1: U.S. power (and for much of the period, predominance); the effects of positive political and economic trends, such as democratization, economic liberalization, and technology-fueled productivity growth; and finally, the influence of the postwar order—its institutions, its organizing principles, and the gravitational effect of its value-sharing community of nations.

The resulting causal model therefore emphasizes the *complementarity among variables* rather than the unique effect of one factor alone. It readily acknowledges that the postwar order was only possible, and was only associated with the positive political and economic outcomes of the postwar era, because it aligned with the effects of U.S. power and broad global trends. Such a causal model can produce few clear-cut statistical findings: The relationships are too complex and the variables too numerous to allow easily measurable conclusions. But a combination of empirical evidence, case studies, and expert validation suggests that the various components of the order have had important value in legitimizing and strengthening U.S. influence and institutionalizing and accelerating the positive trends.[3] One such example is reflected in the text box that describes the ways in which a shared order creates a legitimizing mantle for U.S. power and reduces the degree of power balancing against the United States.

This approach does create significant challenges, however, when attempting to measure the value of the order on its own terms in objec-

---

[2]   Lisa Martin and Beth Simmons have argued that "productive new lines of research emerge if we accept that institutions are *simultaneously causes and effects*; that is, institutions are both the objects of state choice and consequential" (Martin and Simmons, 1998, p. 743). That is precisely the approach we take in this study, viewing the postwar institutional order as fully designed to serve existing state interests—but important nonetheless. We are interested not so much in whether the order has value in a generic sense, and we have looked for evidence suggesting how specific elements of order, or the order as a whole, have done so. This distinction is made in Hafner-Burton, von Stein, and Gartzke (2008, pp. 176, 179–180).

[3]   See, for example, Ruggie, 1982, pp. 381–383.

Figure 3.1
Postwar International Politics: Explanatory Variables

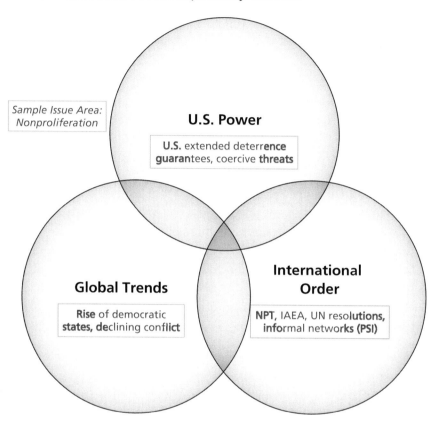

NOTES: NPT = Treaty on the Non-Proliferation of Nuclear Weapons; IAEA = International Atomic Energy Agency; PSI = Proliferation Security Initiative.
RAND RR2226OSD-3.1

tive, quantifiable terms. We deal with this challenge in three ways, an approach reflected in each of the major sections that follow on categories of value. First, we have reviewed, and this report cites a number of examples of, the extensive empirical literature that traces specific effects to key institutions of the order, such as alliances or the General Agreement on Tariffs and Trade (GATT) and World Trade Organization (WTO). Second, we offer cases of the basic dynamic outlined earlier—the way in which elements of the order work hand in glove with other factors to produce beneficial outcomes.

Legitimizing U.S. Power—and Forestalling Hard Balancing

Henry Kissinger argued in his most recent book, *World Order*, that "any system of world order, to be sustainable, must be accepted as just."[4] Power without moral legitimacy will create antibodies and eventually fail; morality without power is ineffectual. It was partly out of recognition of this fact that the architects of the postwar U.S. national security strategy embedded U.S. power in a shared order: They created a justification for the United States to undertake a global leadership role. U.S. power has been legitimized by the purpose of a shared multilateral order.

The result has arguably been one of the cardinal reasons that the order confers a competitive advantage on the United States: For much of the postwar world, it has been viewed as operating in service of the values and norms of the order. The United States stands for something beyond the exercise of power, something of tangible benefit to other countries—a claim that competitors such as China cannot make.

This legitimizing function has had very specific benefits for the United States. Most notably, it has meant that, even throughout most of the post–Cold War period of U.S. predominance and the absence of other threats, few if any states have perceived a need to undertake classic balancing of American power. The reason, as the political scientist Robert A. Pape explains, is not merely a U.S. preponderance of power in classic realist terms. It is that "until recently the United States enjoyed a robust reputation for nonaggressive intentions toward major powers and lesser states beyond its own hemisphere. Although it has fought numerous wars, the United States has generally used its power to preserve the established political order in major regions of the world, seeking to prevent other powers from dominating rather than seeking to dominate itself."[5] Nesting its power in the justifying context of a shared order has

---

[4] Kissinger, 2014, p. 8.

[5] Pape, 2005, pp. 9, 18–21.

potentially saved the United States tens of billions of dollars in additional defense expenditures that would have been necessary—and possibly hundreds of billions of dollars needed to fight additional wars—had other leading states sought to balance its power more aggressively.

Third and most speculatively, we have attempted to assign specific return-on-investment values to ten sample activities or outcomes associated with the order. In order to do this, we have identified, in each major area, several examples of issues or events on which the institutional framework, specific processes of multilateral coordination or active cooperation, or the dominant core group of states of the order has come into play: for example, the global reaction to Saddam Hussein's 1990 aggression against Kuwait or the collective response to the 2008 financial crisis. We then offer a very limited suggestion of a counterfactual case: What might have happened in the absence of the institutions, multilateral sensibility, and core coalition of the order? Finally, we examine potential costs of the difference between the two. These estimates are necessarily based on judgment, but they provide at least an entry point to understanding the return on investment provided by the order.

Another complication is that various institutions of the order have differing records of success. Some, such as the UN Human Rights Council, have proved highly problematic. Others, such as the IMF and World Bank, can point to numerous successes—but also provoke a spirited debate about the overall effect of their policies. No single verdict can encompass the varying outcomes produced by distinct institutions. We have kept such constraints on the available evidence firmly in mind in our review of the potential value of the order.

CHAPTER FOUR
How Do Orders Have Impact?

In order to measure the value of the postwar order, we drew on work from an earlier report in this project to conceive how orders *may* theoretically achieve effects and add value.[1] Drawing on research in political science and political theory, that report suggested four such mechanisms, summarized here. Empirical work and theory in political science suggest that orders can have value in a number of powerful ways.

One is by providing a mechanism to allow functional, rationally directed cooperation on issues of common interest. Especially in an increasingly interlinked global system, states naturally have a growing number of shared interests and goals, from economic stability to environmental health. Institutions can serve this function in a number of ways—they can "lengthen the shadow of the future, facilitate linkages, and monitor and implement agreements."[2] This version of the role of institutions has been called "contractual institutionalism" or "rational functionalism" and is a narrower and less idealistic way of conceiving the role of institutions.[3] Such institutions can facilitate cooperation through a host of mechanisms: reducing transaction costs of cooperation, defining coordination points where collaboration can occur,[4] building physical capabilities to tackle problems or share information,

---

[1] Mazarr, Priebe, Radin, and Cevallos, 2016.

[2] Rathbun, 2011, p. 243.

[3] Weiss, 2015, p. 1222.

[4] Martin and Simmons, 1998, pp. 744–745.

creating habits and expectations of reciprocity,[5] and promoting learning by member states and participating individuals.[6]

Second, international orders gain much of their power by building on domestically grounded interests in the member states. In this sense an order is an outgrowth of state interests, not the cause of them.[7] It should therefore come as little surprise that international orders can achieve effects in the way that they become integrated with domestic interests and interest groups.[8] International institutions can project their influence through domestic constituencies in a number of specific ways.[9] They can infuse beliefs and norms, affect the standard operating procedures of domestic agencies, serve as rallying points for domestic interest groups to advance their positions, and become integrated into domestic law.

Third and in a longer-term sense, the institutional order can also have effects through socialized norms, beliefs, and taken-for-granted understandings in shaping behavior.[10] Our assessment of the value of international order does not presume a "strong" version of the socialization hypothesis. That is, we do not assume that international interactions automatically produce positive socialization effects with decisive influence over state preferences or behavior. Nonetheless, there is strong empirical support for some degree of socialization as a by-product of a shared order. By shaping the essential worldviews and preferences of key actors, socialization processes represent arguably the most powerful long-term influence an order can have.[11]

---

[5] Regimes do not substitute for fundamental perception of reciprocity but can "reinforce and institutionalize it." They can "delegitimize defection and thereby make it more costly" (Axelrod and Keohane, 1985, in Oye, 1986, pp. 249–250).

[6] Martin and Simmons, 1998, p. 735.

[7] Haggard and Simmons, 1987, pp. 499, 515–517.

[8] Martin and Simmons, 1998, pp. 732, 735, 738; Moravcsik, 1997, p. 537. For an EU-specific analysis of this model, see Walsh, 2001.

[9] Cortell and Davis, 1996.

[10] Checkel, 2005, p. 804.

[11] Ikenberry and Kupchan, 1990.

Research over the last several decades has produced impressive evidence for the effects of socialization processes. As Alastair Iain Johnston has argued, some degree of socialization is almost inevitable when actors participate in shared institutions. They simply cannot emerge without being altered in some way.[12] Empirical studies demonstrate the effect on opinion over time.[13] Studies have pointed to the effect of socialization within specific countries integrating into the order, particularly China.[14] Key elements of international law have become socialized as taken-for-granted processes and principles.[15]

Fourth and finally, there is a rich theoretical literature on the systemic effects that can arise in international politics. One is the emergence of a critical mass of roughly aligned countries with disproportionate global influence. This effect is most pronounced in economic affairs: If countries representing a dominant component of global GDP form an economic order, as occurred after 1945, other countries will face a simple choice of joining or losing out on the world's leading markets and sources of capital. When combined with conditions for joining the core group, this situation can affect preferences and behavior: A functioning international order does not change interests but can shape the context for states' deciding on the best strategies to achieve them. There is therefore the potential for a "massive gravitational sphere" at the heart of the postwar order—one that, as the text box that follows suggests, helps to establish a favorable reference point for national competition.[16]

---

[12] Johnston, 2001. See also Buzan, 1993, p. 335; the emergence of rules, he argues, inevitably produces some degree of international society.

[13] Bearce and Bondanella, 2007.

[14] Johnston, *Social States* (2007), offers an in-depth analysis of this socialization effect in China.

[15] "As transnational actors interact," Harold Koh has argued, "they create patterns of behavior that ripen into institutions, regimes, and transnational networks." These interactions produce norms that become internalized in domestic law and fully "enmeshed" with international legal regimes. See Koh, 1996–1997, p. 2654.

[16] Snyder, 2013a, p. 219.

Establishing the Reference Point for Competition

Our research suggests that the postwar order has played an especially critical role in shaping the behavior of states by creating the reference point for national competitive advantage. Our evaluation of the order's value did not begin with an assumption of natural affinity of interests among states. If states are seeking relative advantage in a competitive international system, what role can the institutions, norms, and rules of a shared order play in shaping their preferences and behavior?

One way in which they can do so is by *defining the nature of competition*, an effect that we find evident in both statements of leaders and governments of major powers and the behavior of those states, especially since the late 1980s. Put simply, *the postwar order has shaped the lens through which states interpret the requirements of effective rivalry.* Through a combination of a dominant gravitational core in the international economy and a critical mass of leading, value-sharing democracies, and through the association of both with a limited but specific set of firm rules (such as nonaggression) and long-term aspirations (such as liberal values), the order has laid out the necessary direction for states hoping to compete effectively. States must join international economic institutions, participate in global markets, gain access to capital and technology, undertake reforms to provide good governance, and avoid blatant violations of several key norms. One example comes from the ranking systems set up by international institutions—they become the focus of competition, with national leaders hoping to move up the lists.

As in all of these measures of value, the postwar order has not had this effect alone. The requirements for effective competition have also been demonstrated by long-term evidence for the innovative and adaptive value of liberal societies, for example, and have been affected by advances in technology. But the order—the gravitational core of leading, value-sharing market economies; global networks of finance and business; and the thick web of rules and institutions that govern international economic exchanges—has played a critical role in defining the avenues to national prosperity. In this way, the postwar order shapes the preferences of states seeking relative competitive advantage.

There is abundant evidence that these aspects of the order have affected state behavior. The evidence emerges in the statements of senior leaders endorsing the essential message of interlinked economies—such as Chinese president Xi Jinping's 2017 comments at Davos. It comes from national economic behavior as states integrate into trading regimes. It comes from dozens of cases of reforms undertaken to align state governance and economic standards with the global demands. And in the broadest sense, it emerges in the long-term positive trends in areas such as trade integration and rule of law.

Another systemic effect is related but distinct: The role of status considerations and mutual recognition can provide an important constraint on behavior.[17] States seek status for a number of reasons, partly for power considerations (because high status levels are assumed to be associated with greater influence) but also for reasons of pride and prestige.[18] The gravitational pull of an order can achieve part of its effect through this mechanism: A state acquires status and prestige by being a member in good standing of the prevailing order. As the preceding text box suggests, a coherent international order establishes the reference point for competition, and in so doing sets key standards against which states will be judged in the assessment of their status, and thus achieves some degree of leverage over the preferences and behavior of those states. The regimes and institutions of such an order can also "help to facilitate cooperation by making it both easier and more desirable to acquire a good reputation."[19]

---

[17] Johnston, 2001, p. 492; Keohane, 2002, p. 8; Larson and Shevchenko, 2010. See also Lebow, 2014.

[18] Johnston, 2001, pp. 490, 500–501.

[19] Axelrod and Keohane, 1985, in Oye, 1986, p. 250. The other side of this coin is the urge to avoid stigma, or a perception of deviance from international norms.

As with all the theoretical ways in which order can influence state preferences and behavior, there are limits to this effect. Status considerations cannot explain many actions of states that sometimes flout international norms in ways that will impair, not enhance, their membership-based prestige.[20] Status considerations in regard to membership groups always compete with self-defined interests. In order for reputational effects to work, moreover, participants in an order have to understand what counts as rule breaking.[21] Nor is it clear that this unifying effect will survive the transition to a more multipolar order: China, Russia, and others intent on greater influence are attempting to establish competing institutions, norms, and rules as a legitimate basis for status and legitimacy.

Taken together, these mechanisms provide important ways in which an order can come to reflect a whole whose impact is significantly greater than the sum of its parts. The question is to what degree the actual postwar order has realized these theoretical possibilities. That is the topic to which we now turn.

---

[20] See, for example, Betts, 2012.

[21] Johnston, 2001, pp. 501–502.

CHAPTER FIVE

Measuring Value: International Economic Issues

Measuring the value of the postwar institutional order demands an appreciation of the goals the United States has sought in regard to that order. Elements of order are best viewed as means, not ends: They are tools that can serve U.S. and shared international interests. It is critical to understand the nature of U.S. objectives when evaluating the effectiveness of elements of order in promoting them.

For the purposes of this study, looking at the history of order-building projects beginning in the 1940s, we have argued that the United States has sought four leading objectives. These are the benchmarks against which we measure the order's value:

- *Promote prosperity by creating a supportive context of trade and financial integration, economic stability, and development.* Both the order's geopolitical components and its economic institutions have encouraged the prosperity of participating states in various ways, from encouraging trade integration to stabilizing financial markets.
- *Prevent major power conflict and manage competition.* The order must provide a mechanism to integrate and moderate the policies of major powers that might otherwise end up as revisionists—and if that effort fails, to deter and contain their ambitions.
- *Facilitate collective action to achieve meaningful progress on shared challenges.* The postwar order has helped to catalyze action in a number of ways: by providing institutions that reduce the transaction costs of cooperation, encouraging the rise of nongovernmental networks of action, and providing overarching normative support for collective action.

- *Promote liberal values and democracy.* Treaties and conventions on human rights, support for democratic institutions, and humanitarian intervention are examples of the postwar order's liberal character.

We assessed the potential value of the order in relation to these four broad objectives, in three issue areas—international economics, international security, and liberal norms and values. Each of the next three chapters examines one of these issue areas, and we begin here with international economics.

Origins and Purpose of the International Economic Order

The postwar institutional order rests on a foundation of core economic institutions, beginning with the GATT and WTO and later including the World Bank and IMF. But the economic order must be conceived in broader ways than mere treaties and institutions. It has also reflected shared views of the global economy and joint goals, such as monetary stability and openness. It has institutionalized and then built on the gravitational force of a core group of liberal market economies. It has spurred and then reflected a dense network of relationships among financial officials and experts, many grounded in ideas developed in similar schools and postings. These more informal bonds have often been as important in achieving tangible results as formal institutional pathways.

The postwar economic institutions were designed to underwrite a vision of nondiscriminatory, liberalized trade and to provide consultative processes and mechanisms that would stabilize flows of trade and capital. Christina L. Davis and Meredith Wilf have argued that "those who created the post–World War II trade regime sought to establish rules that would prevent the kind of breakdown of the economic order that occurred in the 1930s."[1] Partly as a result, this postwar institutional order also reflected a growing normative momentum, first within the West and then globally, for the superiority of liberal economic systems. That trend never produced a complete

---

[1]   Davis and Wilf, 2015, p. 380.

agreement; rebellions against the liberalizing demands of the "Washington Consensus," and the IMF's often austerity-based conditions for financial support, have been a consistent feature of international economic affairs since 1945. The order's leading states never embraced a totally liberal or laissez-faire approach but rather reached a compromise designed to achieve substantial free trade while still respecting key domestic interests.[2]

There are therefore limits to the sources of value for the postwar economic order. Some scholars perceive the postwar economic institutions as ineffective because they have not been able to prevent catastrophic international or multinational financial crises.[3] Another common critique of the IMF and World Bank is that they often "get it wrong," meaning that their policy guidance has in several cases proved to be misguided—particularly on the subjects of privatization and liberalization of financial markets.[4] Empirical studies have generated mixed evidence about whether trade regimes alone have boosted levels of trade among participating states[5] or enhanced economic output among participating states.[6] These debates are extensive and intense, and we could not begin to resolve them for the purposes of this analysis. We therefore must look at evidence for and against the value of the international economic order independent of a fundamental verdict on the efficacy of the IMF or the World Bank.

Even with this qualification, our research indicates that the postwar order has had significant economic value, working alongside the other dominant postwar trends. "Multilateralism," the economist

---

[2] This is the essential compromise that Ruggie refers to as "embedded liberalism." See Ruggie, 1982, pp. 385–388.

[3] Helleiner, 2010, p. 629.

[4] Bhargava, 2008, p. 405. See also Milner, 2005, pp. 833–837; and Barro and Lee, 2003. They contend that participation in IMF programs depresses growth, investment, the rule of law, and democracy.

[5] A. Rose, "Do We Really Know That the WTO Increases Trade?," National Bureau of Economic Research Working Paper 9273, October 2004. Rose's work has sparked a wide range of responses, but the debate is sufficiently balanced that we do not include increased trade as a central value measure of the postwar order.

[6] For a recent argument in favor of welfare gains but that cites contrary literature, see Ganelli and Tervala, 2015.

Anne O. Krueger has argued, "has been the key to the huge economic successes of the past half-century."[7] Table 5.1 describes the specific contributions of the postwar order in the context of other variables— such as the domestic economic, trade, and monetary policies of states; the productivity gains from technology; and U.S. influence—to help underwrite growth and trade in ways that have served U.S. interests.[8] The components of the order are not uniquely responsible for these benefits, but they have played an essential supporting role.

Lowering Trade Barriers and Forestalling Protectionist Outcomes

The architects of the postwar order had one leading purpose in mind: avoiding the self-interested, beggar-thy-neighbor protectionism that had helped to bring on the Great Depression.[9] In service of this concern, the economic order's various agreements, beginning with the GATT, have created a treaty framework for lowering tariffs and nontariff barriers among participating networks. The baseline goal of the postwar economic order—forestalling new rounds of self-destructive trade behavior such as competitive devaluations and tariffs—has been achieved. As economics professor Richard E. Baldwin has concluded, the GATT's initial purpose was "to establish a rules-based world trading system and to facilitate mutually advantageous trade liberalization. . . . Both goals have largely been achieved," with the rule-based WTO system now "almost universally accepted and respected by its 163 members" and tariffs on average below 5 percent on most trade. "In the main, the WTO can claim 'mission accomplished,'"[10] in terms of establishing a shared international economic order whose rules help stabilize patterns of trade and other forms of economic interaction.

---

[7] Krueger, 2006.

[8] We include such a table in each of the following sections to explicitly recognize the manner in which the elements of international order work alongside other factors.

[9] A brief history of the series of protectionist surges that characterized the late 19th century through the 1920s can be found in World Trade Organization, 2007, pp. 35–49.

[10] Baldwin, 2016, pp. 95, 111.

Table 5.1
Value of the International Order: International Economics

U.S. Objectives[a]

- National prosperity in part through stable and fair global economic system
- Strong global growth rates
- Free trade and global trade integration
- Progress in less developed areas
- Avoid and mitigate economic crises

Contributing Factors

Leading Trends
- Technology advances aiding productivity
- Neoliberal reforms in key economies accompanied by supporting fiscal and monetary policies
- Population growth in developing countries

Role of U.S. Power
- Attractive and coercive role of desired access to the dominant U.S. market
- U.S. leverage and coercion promoting liberal reforms
- U.S. extended deterrence guarantees and military presence providing stability in key regions and setting the stage for growth

Elements of the Postwar Order
- A stable trading regime, including lowered trade barriers from global, regional, and bilateral treaties
- Interaction with domestic interest groups to promote liberal economic values
- Institutional and normative engines of effective response to economic crises
- Efficiency and innovation gains through standards, agreements, and networks
- Material and nonmaterial attraction of the predominant economic core

Evidence for Effects of Order

- Quantified tariff and nontariff barrier reduction; mixed but still significant evidence for increased global trade
- Use and compliance rate of WTO dispute mechanism
- Role of institutions, and case studies of national attitudes, in responding to crises
- Reforms undertaken by aspirants desiring membership in order's institutions (WTO, NAFTA, EU, etc.)
- Qualitative assessment of effect of gravitational core of order

NOTES: NAFTA = North American Free Trade Agreement; EU = European Union.

[a]We recognize a complex cause-and-effect relationship among a number of these goals. Many of them can be considered sub-sets of the first, most fundamental objective, of national prosperity. But each of the others listed here have other purposes as well: Global growth helps ease the basis for civil conflict and protectionism, for example, and trade integration promotes interdependence.

The order has played a useful role in preserving these gains.[11] During economic downturns, states perceive powerful incentives to pursue seemingly self-interested trade restrictions. In order to prevent such a cascade of protectionism during lean times, "an international economic regime underpinning and enforcing multilateralism in international transactions is vital."[12] There is some evidence, in fact, that during post-1945 crisis periods, states imposed fewer protectionist measures than would have been expected given historical experience.[13]

An institutionalized order can achieve these results in a number of ways. Beyond their specific requirements in terms of tariff reductions and other trade openings, these agreements—measured in terms such as reduced tariff barriers and active collaboration to resolve problems—have had important signaling effects. They pointed to a shared direction and rallied leading economic powers to pursue liberalization.[14] The principles of the postwar economic order "fostered a self-reinforcing pattern of cooperation and success."[15]

---

[11] The economic journalist Paul Blustein, generally skeptical of the role of international institutions, nonetheless concludes, based on extensive dialogues with global economic officials, that "for all its faults, the WTO is a crucial linchpin of stability in the global economy" and continues to play its critical role as "the current embodiment of the multilateral system that was established after World War II to prevent a reversion to the trade policies of the thirties." Blustein, 2009, p. 11.

[12] Krueger, 2006.

[13] See, for example, Germain, 2009, p. 677, who, regarding the basic principles of free trade and market function in the wake of the 2008 financial crisis, argues that "what is interesting about all the discussions surrounding how to fix the world's financial system and upgrade its associated regulatory apparatus is that nowhere are these principles being directly challenged."

[14] This is the real importance of the GATT, at least in its early years, suggests Douglas Irwin. His findings actually support doubts about the connection between trade agreements and levels of trade: The accord "does not appear to have stimulated a particularly rapid liberalization of world trade in the decade after 1947," he suggests. After an initial bout of limited tariff reduction, the "GATT's momentum suddenly stalled," and even the tariff reductions that were accomplished were limited in their effect by other trade restrictions. "One is left with tremendous uncertainty about the precise role of the GATT in promoting economic recovery in Western Europe in the first decade after the war." And yet the GATT did have two important benefits: It "set standards for state behavior which . . . at least created a reference point about the direction in which trade policies should be heading." Giving the goal of liberalization "an institutional basis" helped to prevent "a drift in economic policies away" from those principles. Irwin 1994, pp. 127–128, 148.

[15] Baldwin, 2016, p. 106.

The Overarching Effect of Order: Producing a Self-Reinforcing Equilibrium

Many analyses of the postwar order's effects focus on single institutions—asking whether an alliance deters war or a trade agreement boosts levels of trade. One of the main findings of our research is that an issue-specific lens does not capture the most important role of international orders. Their dominant effect emerges through broader causal mechanisms. One is that, through their agreements, rules, norms, and institutions, they establish a prevailing pattern or equilibrium that shapes expectations.

Dynamic equilibrium holds when negative feedback factors within an ecosystem are powerful enough to obstruct major transformations. Such situations can be affected by the inputs to the reactions—the nature of the reactants. When systems are placed under stress, the behavior of their constituent parts changes, and equilibrium can be upset. Change, which is gradual and incremental under a dynamic equilibrium, can become sudden, discontinuous, and devastating.

In this sense, the postwar order has contributed to an imperfect but still important form of dynamic equilibrium in which actors generally behave in constrained ways. The leading example is in the economic sphere. The interlocking set of trade agreements put in place after 1945, and the deepening process of global trade and economic integration and collaboration, has contributed to an emergent sense of a shared economic fate, the need to cooperate in dealing with recessions and crises through such means as coordinated monetary policy, and the inability of nations to prosper in opposition to these established norms. The result is a form of equilibrium that has contributed in limited but important ways to long-term stability or improvement in many economic measures. This equilibrium is being challenged in powerful ways today but remains an important legacy of the postwar economic order.

Such an equilibrium can have influence on potential causes of conflict by reducing the uncertainty inherent in the international system. Uncertainty, especially about the intentions of other states, is a major engine of the security dilemma that drives conflict.[16] International orders mitigate this danger by furnishing greater predictability through their many institutions, rules, and norms. And the equilibrium that can emerge plays an especially crucial role in this sense by offering an expectation of predictable patterns of behavior.

This effect can be difficult to measure, because it embodies the combination of so many factors. We find evidence for it, however, in a number of places:

- repeated and consistent statements about the essential norms of the order, including nonaggression and cooperative security, from national leaders and senior officials
- long-term stability in key measures of the status of the order in such areas as trade openness, economic freedom, transparency and corruption, and conflict
- the documented role of key institutions, treaties, and norms in dampening the potentially disruptive effects of crises and disputes.

The effect of such a dynamic equilibrium may be especially powerful in economic terms, where the self-interest of nations in the preservation of stability is especially strong. In the case of trade, research suggests that the multilateral regime put in place after 1945 created a commitment to tariff reduction that has established an equilibrium, one that has survived a number of major economic crises.[17] The dense network of trade and economic institutions, treaties, and norms creates an absorptive capacity to deal with negative feedback, dampening the possible implications of trade disputes and economic crises. This equilibrium has been of significant value to the United States.

---

[16] See, for example, Rathbun, 2007.

[17] See, for example, Clemens and Williamson, 2004.

This established direction then gave a solid policy direction for states to trust, reducing uncertainty. Under what is known as "commitment theory," one purpose of trade agreements is to provide stable expectations of future returns to capital. This reduces the premium on constantly shifting investments into different sectors, preventing trade flows from becoming more erratic over time.[18] One study supported the hypothesis of "self-enforcing" trade agreements based on the idea of mutual interest: Once locked into a beneficial trade regime, states hesitate to undertake large-scale protectionism because of the expectation of retaliation and the loss of benefits.[19] There is significant evidence that global and regional trade agreements have indeed had these effects, providing rallying points for states to make commitments that they then must follow, helping to lock in trade gains. Research on NAFTA has similarly found that its institutionalized legal structure has helped to stabilize trade relations and disputes.[20]

The initial and foundational economic benefit of the postwar order, then, has been to institutionalize a relatively nondiscriminatory trade regime that has both created the opportunity of gains through trade and, even more importantly, avoided a descent into widespread protectionism, especially during economic crises. Elements of protectionist and mercantilist behavior continue, and from time to time, especially during severe recessions, states have felt the need to reach for protectionist measures. But the order—working alongside U.S. influence and the consultative role of a predominant set of major trading states—has constrained these bouts with trade restrictions and contributed to a broadly stable global economic system.

The outcome of the postwar economic approach was "a quarter-century-long period of rapid economic growth, greatly outperforming any prior period of comparable length in world economic history."[21]

---

[18] Staiger and Tabellini, 1999. See also Staiger, 2004; Mansfield and Reinhardt, 2008; and Vannoorenberghe, 2012.

[19] Bown and Crowley, 2013.

[20] F. Abbott, 2000. This is distinct from stabilizing amounts or trends in trade; see A. Rose, 2005.

[21] Krueger, 2006.

This result has many causes, not all of them related to the postwar economic order. But that order can be seen as a *necessary*, if not sufficient, condition for this economic boom: It provided the basis for the accelerating trade that was a primary catalyst of growth, it helped to spread the open economic policies that underwrote growth, and it avoided discriminatory trade and economic policies that would have functioned as a drag on the system.

Mutually Reinforcing Interaction with Domestic Interests

Another mechanism by which the postwar economic order has been able to accomplish its goals is in the way it has interacted with domestic interest groups to encourage liberalization and good governance. Domestic policy actors use international norms to advance their interests.[22] One study found that domestic politics, rather than ideas or norms, is more responsible for converging interests and preferences that led to European monetary union behavior in the 1980s.[23] Specifically in economic terms, this is a critical and well-demonstrated effect of trade agreements—to help national governments justify reforms aimed at acceding to the treaties, ward off domestic interests opposed to the reforms, and then lock in those changes over time.

One example is NAFTA's role in encouraging and then locking in cementing reforms in Mexico. "NAFTA has been the fundamental anchor," the head of the North American Development Bank has argued, "for reforms that make Mexico a more modern economy and open society."[24] Another example is IMF agreements, which some research suggests have been used to justify domestic reform pack-

---

[22] Martin and Simmons, 1998, p. 732.

[23] Walsh, 2001.

[24] Quoted in Knowledge@Wharton, "NAFTA's Impact." See also Noland et al., 2016, 43, which concludes that NAFTA and Mexico's accession to the Organization for Economic Cooperation and Development "have served as 'external anchors' establishing international norms for Mexico's reforms and encouraging the modernization of the country's economic institutions."

ages.[25] The same pattern has emerged globally—domestic interests that stand to benefit from free trade and nondiscriminatory economic principles have used the existence of the order to gain clout within their own countries. The result has been to spread the effects of international rules into the domestic spheres of states.

Avoiding and Dampening Economic and Financial Crises

The combination of the order's defining financial and monetary institutions and the formal and informal networks of coordination and collective action it has encouraged has helped to avoid and mitigate economic crises. This has been true in a number of specific IMF interventions, as well as some more systemic ones, such as the halting but eventually significant responses to the 1997 Asian financial crisis.[26] One prominent example of crisis avoidance came in Brazil in 2002, as noted in the following text box.

The most recent example is the behavior of leading countries during the 2008 financial crisis. Daniel Drezner has chronicled numerous elements of the global institutional response to the crisis. He concludes that "despite initial shocks that were more severe than those of the 1929 financial crisis, global economic governance responded in a nimble and robust fashion in 2008."[27] Key evidence for an effective response includes the following:[28]

- In terms of outcomes and effects, despite the fact that the initial drop was steeper in 2008, the recovery of the global economy was much more rapid than in 1929.[29]

---

[25] Vreeland, 2003.

[26] See, for example, Burton, 2007.

[27] Drezner, *The System Worked*, p. 14.

[28] These points are drawn from Drezner, *The System Worked*, pp. 31–38, 41–46, 140–141, 54.

[29] See also Eichengreen and O'Rourke, 2010; and Eichengreen and O'Rourke, 2012. In their later post, they do admit that the recovery slowed significantly after two years and that policy responses to promote continued growth were lagging.

- Levels of global trade recovered relatively quickly and never dropped to the levels seen after the 1929 Depression. There was much less outright beggar-thy-neighbor protectionism. Drezner contends that institutions of economic governance "played a significant role in this outcome," specifically through the constraining effects of WTO membership, consultations in the G-20, and other means.
- Central banks coordinated their activities to offer stimulus to flagging economies and ease capital flows during the crisis.
- The IMF undertook more than $140 billion in new lending to inject stimulus into almost 20 countries.
- Through the G-20, governments consulted on plans for economic stimulus and spent over $2 trillion in 2008 and 2009 to fight the depressing effects of the recession.
- In the wake of the crisis, international financial regulators introduced new rules, in the Basel III program, designed to prevent a recurrence of the crisis. Many experts found them to be inadequate, but they have made a difference—especially the revised capital requirements for banks, which offer the soundest buffer against financial crises.
- The United States and China offered important joint leadership during the crisis, demonstrating that U.S. global influence remains quite considerable and that China was prepared to act as a responsible steward of the international economy.

The economist Andrew K. Rose agrees that the IMF responded rapidly and decisively to the crisis. It sought and received hundreds of billions of dollars in extra lending and pursued a response strategy that avoided the significant criticisms of its rough conditionality during the Asian financial crisis of 1997. And the IMF's role "understates the development of the institutional fabric of the international economy," since new initiatives such as the Financial Stability Forum have added to the world community's response capability and the G-20 emerged as a meaningful actor at several effective conferences during the crisis. At the same time, the underlying norms of the order, including open and non-discriminatory trade, prevented large-scale recourse to protectionism or predatory exchange rate policies, which consistently appeared in earlier

International Institutions Working for U.S. Interests: The IMF in Brazil

During 2002 and early 2003, the Brazilian economy stood on the brink of default, in part because some of the candidates for president in the upcoming elections were promising economic policies that risked capital exodus. Brazil held over $260 billion in external debt, and a default would have had major global implications, perhaps sparking a contagion effect similar to the Asian financial crisis of the 1990s.

Stepping in to avert an imminent default, the IMF provided a loan of over $30 billion, which stabilized the Brazilian economy and "arguably helped avert a meltdown that would have slammed global markets from Manila to Istanbul."[30] The result held very specific advantages for the United States. U.S. banks held significant amounts of Brazilian debt, and bank stocks—and then the whole stock market—rose on news of the bailout. U.S. auto manufacturers had made significant investments in factories in Brazil and praised the stabilizing result. In Latin America, "stock markets in Brazil, Chile and even Argentina jumped briskly. Brazil's battered currency, the real, strengthened nearly 4 percent against the dollar."[31] Meanwhile, the George W. Bush administration used the program as a lever to extract promises of continued respect for IMF requirements from the various presidential candidates. By March 2005, Brazil was able to end its IMF agreement, having survived the scare and avoided a much more serious economic price.

Even this IMF program was hardly perfect. Brazil has since 2005 slid into a new economic crisis from which it is struggling to extricate itself. Many underlying socioeconomic challenges remain unresolved. But the 2002 assistance package provides a specific example of cases in which the international economic order has avoided significantly worse outcomes and thereby supported U.S. interests.

---

[30] Rogoff, 2006. See also International Monetary Fund, 2007.

[31] Andrews, 2002.

crises.[32] At least in one case, we might reasonably argue that the institutions and norms of the international order proved resilient, especially as compared to historical parallels.

Improving International Economic Coordination, Efficiency, and Innovation

The postwar economic architecture has offered numerous mechanisms to facilitate dialogue and information exchange and to coordinate policies. The institutions have reduced the transaction costs of cooperation and provided ready-made and widely supported avenues for such coordination.

One example of such a mechanism is the twice-annual meeting of finance ministers, central bankers, and corporate and nongovernmental organization (NGO) heads that occurs under the auspices of the IMF and World Bank.[33] These meetings provide a venue for sharing information and discussing options for promoting economic stability and growth. But their existence also prompts a range of bilateral meetings to prepare for them, and the meeting has served as a model for a number of regional counterpart gatherings. In this way, a modest institution of international economic governance has significant spin-off effects in global governance.

Another important though often overlooked role of international economic institutions is to create a shared, rigorous, objective pool of economic data that can be used to assess the state of the global economy and design responses. Once states see where they rank on various indices, their leadership can respond with competitive drives to enhance their standing. This effect has emerged dozens of times—national leaders or their key economic officials stating a determination to join the top ranks of global countries on some key metric, ranging from infant mortality to transparency to credit ratings. In this sense an objective global set of data becomes the fuel for the gravitational effects of the order.

---

[32] A. Rose, 2010.

[33] See International Monetary Fund, 2017.

The agreements and rules of the postwar economic order in the area of international finance have also helped to produce more-coherent and more-effective international financial markets. Financial regulatory harmonization is not straightforward or always efficient, Beth Simmons has found, but follows interactions between what she terms a "regulatory innovator" and the broader financial markets.[34] The postwar economic order has included a wide range of issue- and discipline-specific institutions, norms, and practices that have helped to produce more-efficient economic relationships. These include transnational standards and professional groups in areas such as economics, accounting, finance, supply chain management, and more.[35]

In the process, the order's dense network of state and nonstate institutions, rules, and norms has helped to facilitate economic relations and made business transactions more efficient, thus promoting growth and offering more opportunities for such positive outcomes as business innovation and supply chain efficiencies. These detailed, issue-specific agreements could have taken place without a larger order, but they would have been less likely. In the process, postwar economic institutions have created mobilization points around which domestic interests favoring liberalized trade and integrated economic systems have been able to rally.

Building a Normative Basis for Stability and Growth

Finally and most fundamentally in the long term, the sum total of the economic order's norms, rules, and institutions has created expectations and habits that stabilize the international economy, providing a sort of "institutional glue" that has helped hold the world economy together.[36] The existence of an order with shared and understood rules

---

[34] Simmons, 2001.

[35] For a study of one of these areas, see Arnold, 2009.

[36] Former World Bank head Robert Zoellick has argued that institutions play an important role in such a process; apart from their discrete functions, they "also shape ideas" and "play a policy and catalytic role" (Ansley, 2017).

and objectives has changed the preference calculus for states considering mercantilist behavior. Given the overwhelming predominance of the core group of value-sharing democracies, and the role of linked markets and investment firms making decisions based in part on geopolitical risk, states would have more difficulty achieving sustained economic growth without access to the capital, technology, expertise, and markets of this core group—and thus are subject to its conditions for membership.

Another way in which an institutionalized order spreads these norms is through the thousands of networks that exist among economists and economic policy officials. In global economic conferences, both official and unofficial; Track 2 dialogues; the rotational assignment of national economic officials to international bodies like the IMF and World Bank; regional economic institutions and conferences; and hundreds more such interactions, the more diffuse elements of the global order contribute to mutual understanding and lay the groundwork for agreements.

There are limits to this function of the order. States are often more persuaded by material threats and opportunities than by trade norms: One empirical study found that retaliatory threats were more powerful than normative obligations in securing adherence to WTO dispute resolution outcomes.[37] But there is evidence that trade agreements and other elements of the postwar economic order—while perhaps less important in determining outcomes than other economic variables such as macroeconomic policies—have had an important stage-setting function, in large part by defining the broad directions states need to move in order to compete in world politics. They "set standards for state behavior," Douglas Irwin has argued in a study of the GATT, standards that "created a reference point about the direction trade policies should be headed." In a related sense, he argued, the GATT helped ensure that countries would not rush to impose new tariffs and other protectionist measures once the initial round of trade liberalization took hold.[38]

---

[37] Bown, 2004.

[38] Irwin 1994, p. 27.

This broad, precedent-setting, and principle-reinforcing function is arguably the single most important role of the postwar economic order. It created the criteria against which individual economic decisions were judged and kept countries from readily turning to trade-destroying measures during difficult economic periods. The same process has generated a recurring focus on "good governance" and the rule of law as necessary complements to economic integration.[39]

And in this process, the multilateral economic order has played another role for the United States: providing an independent voice advocating for liberal economic policies—and often, taking the heat for those policies. In a range of economic crises since the early 1990s, the IMF has taken the lead in promoting and in some cases enforcing sometimes painful economic measures designed to restore stability to a specific country and prevent a larger destabilization of the international economy. Had it not been available to push the norms of a liberal economic order in difficult times, the United States would likely have had to take the lead in doing so alone or with a small number of countries, exposing itself to the blowback from such interventions. In the promotion of global economic norms, one role for international institutions is therefore to enforce rules and absorb the resulting ire of countries undergoing difficult transitions.

An excellent summary of the benefits of the institutions of a multilateral economic order can be found in a remarkable 1982 study by the Reagan administration's Treasury Department. It highlighted three broad objectives the United States sought to promote in the order: the "development of a more secure and stable world through economic growth"; the promotion of a free and open trading system; and fulfilling a "humanitarian concern with alleviating poverty."[40]

The study, which focused on multilateral development banks (MDBs), concluded that U.S. participation contributed significantly to all three objectives—in addition to reaping side benefits, such as promoting U.S. commercial interests, sharing the burden of global economic stability, and rallying support for U.S. policy goals within the banks.

---

[39] See, for example, Williams 2008.

[40] U.S. Department of the Treasury, 1982, pp. 3–6.

The report concluded that "continued U.S. participation in the MDBs is justified by the fundamental national interest in a more stable and secure world, which we believe can best be achieved in an open, market-oriented international system." By encouraging movement in that direction, these institutions constitute "one of the major vehicles available for pursuing these U.S. economic and political/strategic interests."[41] Our findings suggest that these basic conclusions remain valid in terms of the broader suite of postwar multilateral economic institutions.

Summary: The Economic Value of the Order

The economic benefits of the postwar order are obvious and significant. In some cases, as with trade agreements to reduce tariffs, they have played a role in promoting additional economic prosperity. In other cases, the institutions and norms of the order provided a critical safeguarding role, preventing backsliding in the form of trade wars or competitive monetary policies. In the postwar era, global per capita GDP has shot up fivefold, from about $2,000 to over $10,000; during the same period, U.S. per capita GDP grew substantially as well, from roughly $15,000 to over $50,000. Our research supports the conclusion that, while this incredible leap in global and U.S. prosperity is attributable to many factors, it would not have been possible to the same degree, or with as much consistency, without the institutions, rules, and norms of the postwar order.

---

[41] U.S. Department of the Treasury, 1982, pp. 3–6.

CHAPTER SIX

Measuring Value: International Security Issues

The components of the postwar order have also contributed to U.S. foreign and national security policy on security-related issues. As Table 6.1 indicates, many factors have been responsible for the period of significant peace since 1945. Our argument is not that the order generated these outcomes on its own. Rather, as in the case of international economics, it has offered a number of specific tools and processes that have significantly enhanced the effect of U.S. strategy.

The Effect of a Predominant Reference Group on the Risk Calculus of Aggression

The first and perhaps most powerful manner in which the order has helped promote peace and security is the way in which the existence of a predominant membership group has changed the calculus of potential aggressors. When an international order links together a predominant set of countries into a broad partnership and even quasi-mutual defense alliance, it can restrain aggression. While specific disputes and aggressive actions may emerge, challenging the whole core coalition in the international system would be infeasible in classic great power terms.

In prior eras, a state coveting its neighbor's territory or resources could often assume that other major powers would cast a blind eye toward aggression, in part because it was an expected tool in world politics. Even if some states might oppose the action, an aggressor could often split a highly varied and fractious set of leading powers,

Table 6.1
Value of the International Order: International Security

U.S. Objectives

- Protecting the homeland
- Avoidance of aggressive wars
- Promoting stability in key regions
- Preserving key norms such as freedom of the commons

Contributing Factors

Leading Trends

- Integrated global market discourages and reduces the value of aggressive warfare
- Rise of democracy creates actors less likely to go to war with one another

Role of U.S. Power

- Global military predominance helps to deter major aggression
- U.S. extended deterrence contribution to alliances helps deter war in key regions
- Training, advisory, assistance, and other roles boost capacity of partner militaries

Elements of the Postwar Order

- The norms and preferences of the core group of states change the risk calculus for potential aggressors
- Military alliances deter regional conflict
- International institutions help avoid or end conflicts or rally responses to aggression
- Peacekeeping activities share burden of global peace enforcement
- Nonproliferation institutions and norms constrain weapons of mass destruction

Evidence for Effects of Order

- Empirical evidence of the effect of alliances
- Level of commitment of other states to peacekeeping activities
- Empirical evidence on relationship between conflict resolution institutions and peace
- Case examples of issues on which institutions catalyze common action or allow the United States to rally support for its goals
- Effect of norms in shaping behavior

ensuring that no dominant balancing force would emerge to confront the attack. The core set of leading status-quo powers at the heart of the current order has altered that dynamic: States considering large-scale aggression now know that they would very likely face significant responses, whether economic, political, or military, from the majority of the world's leading powers. Saddam Hussein discovered this to his surprise in 1990, and Russia has run into a lesser but still powerful degree of the same dynamic since 2014. The institutions, norms, and core community of the order have in this way created a powerful disincentive to major aggression. To be sure, this effect has its limits—the global security coalition is more implicit than explicit, and its willingness to enforce norms at the edges of the order is always in question.

A related systemic effect is the role of status and mutual recognition as a form of constraint on confrontational behavior. A state acquires status and prestige by being a member in good standing of the prevailing order, which employs such status considerations to shape behavior. This effect admits many exceptions—such as states that act in rash or belligerent ways regardless of the status effects. Nonetheless, the postwar order has installed a critical mass of leading states that share a desire to impose a norm of nonaggression and that have few if any unresolved territorial ambitions. States considering large-scale, unprovoked aggression will confront a predominant power bloc opposing the action, in military or nonmilitary terms. This fact about the postwar order has benefited the United States by creating deterrent and shaping effects independent of U.S. power.

The Security Value of Alliances

A second component of the order that has contributed directly to the nonaggression norm has been the network of U.S. alliances, which has served as the centerpiece of the institutional order from the standpoint of national security affairs. Most countries have historically chosen to fight with allies out of a belief that it increases effectiveness.[1] Institutional alliances have arguably allowed the United States to coordinate defense policies more easily with its security partners.

The literature on postwar alliances and the associated forward-deployed posture for U.S. military forces suggests that they have had the following benefits for the United States:

- Both quantitative and case-based evidence suggests that *alliances tend to deter war*.[2] Alliances "have an influence in international politics well beyond collaborative war fighting and deterrence,"

---

[1]   Bensahel, 2007.

[2]   J. Johnson and Leeds, 2011; Leeds, 2003a; Danilovic, 2001.

one recent quantitative analysis concluded. "Alliances deter conflicts, which in itself is a force for peace, but even when challengers are not deterred from making demands, allies can facilitate peaceful settlement. Alliances can be important institutions for conflict management, not only among their members, but between their members and outside states as well. As such, alliances can be broad institutions for peace that play an important role in maintaining the stability of the international system."[3] Alliances and associated forward posturing of U.S. forces deter regional conflict by demonstrating a costly commitment to U.S. friends, providing capabilities needed to deny aggressors' objectives, preventing a quick victory on the part of aggressors, and improving the capabilities of friends and allies.[4]

- *Allies offer host-nation support and direct funding for alliance budgets that significantly complement U.S. defense spending.* America's NATO allies, for example, provide 78 percent of direct alliance funding. South Korea and Japan together provide almost $3 billion annually in direct support of the basing of U.S. forces there. A broader estimate of all categories of host-nation support provided by Japan suggests an annual contribution of $6.5 billion. South Korea is footing $30 billion of the $37 billion bill for new base construction and other costs associated with the bilateral force relocation plan on the peninsula. An overall estimate from one RAND study suggests that, where data is available, allies offset roughly half of the direct U.S. costs of basing.[5]

- *U.S. participation in security alliances provides additional leverage on economic matters.* A recent RAND study argued that the value of the special economic treatment accorded the United States

---

[3]　Fang, Johnson, and Leeds, 2014, p. 2. See also Leeds, 2003b; and Leeds, 1999.

[4]　Lostumbo et al., 2013, pp. 74–86.

[5]　Hicks, Green, and Conley, 2016; Lostumbo et al., 2013, pp. 131–132, 139, 176, and, generally, 131–165.

totaled roughly $490 billion a year in GDP.[6] Other research supports the idea that alliances are associated with trade.[7]

- *Alliances provide an institutional basis for cooperation on emergent issues*, allowing states to undertake rapid responses without re-creating mechanisms of command and control, logistics, and other aspects of coordinated activity.[8] Allies have also provided the United States with support in recent combat deployments, support that might not have been forthcoming without the alliance leverage. Examples include multiple NATO allied commitments to Afghanistan and Iraq, South Korean contributions in Afghanistan, and Japanese naval participation in counterpiracy efforts. U.S. allies have suffered more than 1,000 combat deaths in Afghanistan since 2001.[9]
- *Alliances enhance the capabilities of member nations through such means as interoperability, mutual support, and enhanced training.*[10] NATO has had a number of measurable effects, such as enhancing mutual capabilities.[11]
- *Alliances offer the United States base access for the conduct of regional military operations*, which would be much more difficult, if not impossible, to conduct without such basing access. An extensive RAND analysis showed the value of forward basing and en route basing access to reducing U.S. military costs in such areas as sealift and airlift.[12] These considerations are especially important

---

[6] The study concludes that a 50 percent reduction in U.S. presence could lead to a loss of $577 billion in annual trade, equating to a $490 billion hit to GDP (Egel et al., 2016). See also Brooks and Wohlforth, 2016, p. 93.

[7] Gowa and Mansfield, 1993.

[8] For an argument about this role in the war on terror, see Romaniuk, 2010.

[9] Hicks, Green, and Conley, 2016.

[10] For one example from Saudi Arabia, see Werber, Hanser, and Davis, 2004.

[11] Duffield, 1992, 1994; Moroney, Grissom, and Marquis, 2007; Moroney et al., 2009.

[12] Lostumbo et al., 2013, pp. 40–54. The report contends, "We conclude that without a robust en route infrastructure and lift fleet, rapid global response is not possible" (p. 69).

when dealing with potentially short-notice, fait accompli–style operations—such as a sudden Russian grab of the Baltics—for which the United States would not be able to flow sufficient forces from a distance rapidly enough to deny Russian objectives.

- *Alliances offer the United States institutional means of balancing potential regional hegemons.*[13] The decisive advantage the United States enjoys over China and Russia is the role of allies and partners, which substantially increase our relative military and geopolitical advantage. It is their lack of true allies that provides competitive advantage. Meantime, the argument that alliances entangle the United States in unnecessary wars does not hold up to empirical scrutiny.[14]

This range of evidence suggests that, once the United States made the choice to embrace a strategy of global engagement, alliances provided numerous forms of value and made the process of underwriting global peace and security less costly and risky for the United States.

Norms and Institutions of Conflict Resolution

The postwar order has contributed to peace and security in a third way: through its conflict resolution norms and procedures. There is evidence that intergovernmental or other international organizations produce more peaceful outcomes.[15] The network of institutions built since 1945 is associated with reductions in conflict. Some research distinguishes among international governmental organizations and argues that more-institutionalized ones are positively associated with peace.[16] Another study found that institutions capable of generating strong

---

[13] Medeiros et al., 2008; Bush, 2016.

[14] Beckley, 2015.

[15] This research is summarized in Dorussen and Ward, 2008, pp. 190–191; and Hafner-Burton, von Stein, and Gartzke, 2008, p. 177. See also Russett, Oneal, and Davis, 1998; Simmons, 2002; and Shannon, Morey, and Boehmke, 2010.

[16] Boehmer, Gartzke, and Nordstrom, 2004.

commitments from participating states helped to reduce the length of militarized interstate disputes.[17]

One important recent study, drawing on both theory and empirical assessments of conflict trends, argues that institutions are the critical mechanisms for dampening conflict among democracies.[18] Similar empirical work found that international organizations composed largely of democracies—what scholars call "densely democratic" intergovernmental organizations—are strongly associated with peaceful outcomes.[19]

The role of the United Nations in the U.S.-led response to aggression offers a related example of the helpful role of international institutions in deterring and responding to aggression. Perhaps the leading example of such a role came in 1990–1991, with the global response to Iraq's invasion of Kuwait: The United Nations became the key forum for generating an international consensus on action. Richard Haass was a senior State Department official at the time, and he saw the importance of this role firsthand. "For most people around the world and their governments," he argues, "the UN is an important and at times essential source of authority and legitimacy. Its endorsement can constitute a prerequisite for the participation of others." Properly handled, he argues, multilateralism can be a "force multiplier" for U.S. diplomacy.[20]

Institutional Support for Peacekeeping Operations

Fourth, the institutions, processes, and multilateralism of the order specifically devoted to peacekeeping and peace enforcement operations have relieved burdens on the United States and helped to dampen and end civil wars.[21] Some of these peacekeeping operations (PKOs)

---

[17] Shannon, Morey, and Boehmke, 2010.

[18] Hasenclever and Weiffen, 2006.

[19] Pevehouse and Russett, 2006.

[20] Haass, 2009, pp. 71–72, 196.

[21] Ruggie (1996, pp. 64–70) highlights peacekeeping as one of the leading elements of postwar multilateralism.

have been very high-profile and sometimes obvious failures, as in the minimal United Nations presence in Rwanda before the 1994 geno-cide.[22] But others have been partial or complete successes, and on the whole the institutions that have accomplished this task have offered a significant benefit to the country leading global efforts for stability and security—the United States. PKOs have a range of benefits for U.S. interests: In some cases they support purely humanitarian objec-tives of U.S. foreign policy; in others, as in the Balkans, they have helped to stabilize situations with very significant U.S. strategic inter-ests at stake and avoid the cost and risk of U.S. military intervention.

From 1948 to 2013, the United Nations records 69 UN-led PKOs, from Liberia to the Balkans to East Timor.[23] Some 120 coun-tries have participated in these operations, and over 3,300 peacekeep-ers have died in their service.[24] When regional institutions are added, some 50 to 60 different peacekeeping missions have been under way per year over the last decade. In 2012, not including the UN mission in Afghanistan (which is often counted in peacekeeping numbers), over 130,000 peacekeepers were engaged in ongoing missions.[25] That same year, excluding the Afghan mission, the countries contribut-ing the most troops to PKOs were Pakistan, Bangladesh, India, and several African nations, including Uganda, Ethiopia, and Rwanda.[26] India, Brazil, and China have significantly increased their support to peacekeeping in both financial and manpower terms, and they view PKOs as an important signal of their participation in a shared order.

Despite their limitations and incomplete record of success, these operations have benefited global security and U.S. interests in a number of ways. They have helped to spread the burden of helping to control instability in key regions. The have provided a mechanism for develop-ing nations to fulfill self-perceived global responsibilities and contribute

---

[22] On the modern challenges of peacekeeping and the need for reform, see Gowan, 2014.

[23] The list is in United Nations, n.d.c.

[24] United Nations, n.d.b.

[25] Van der Lijn et al., 2015, pp. 16–17.

[26] Van der Lijn et al., 2015, p. 21.

to a shared order. Countries such as India, Pakistan, and Brazil, which may be skeptical of other elements of global liberal norm building, have come to view PKOs as important symbols of their international commitments. And while the record of post-1948 PKOs is mixed, there is substantial evidence that specific missions have had significant effects on reducing conflict. Empirical studies and literature reviews have demonstrated that peace tends to be more lasting when peacekeepers deploy,[27] that peacekeeping missions reduce civilian deaths when enough peacekeepers are deployed,[28] that societies are less likely to fall back into civil war after peacekeeping missions,[29] and that conflicts tend to spread more readily without peacekeeping interventions.[30]

Nonproliferation Norms and Institutions

A fifth major contribution of the postwar order to security has been through its nonproliferation norms and institutions.[31] They have provided a normative foundation for nonproliferation efforts, specified punishments for states that violate the norms, offered convenient forums for states to reiterate norms and organize their enforcement, and provided institutional support systems such as inspectors and technical experts. As with all elements of the order, they are most properly viewed not as self-contained, self-enforcing rules but rather as "potentially powerful instrument[s] in the U.S. policy toolkit."[32]

An imperfect but still important example comes from the Biological Weapons Convention (BWC). It lacks strongly institutionalized enforcement regimes, and there is no agreed mechanism for reliable

---

[27] For examples of such positive studies, see Fortna, 2004a, 2004b; Gilligan and Sergenti, 2008; Sambanis, 2008; and Paris, 2010, 2014.

[28] Hultman, Kathman, and Shannon, 2013.

[29] Doyle and Sambanis, 2000. See also Doyle and Sambanis, 2006; and Beardsley, 2012.

[30] Beardsley, 2011.

[31] Ruggie, 1996, pp. 70–76.

[32] Tucker, 2001.

verification.[33] There have been a few notable failures, such as Iraq's ability to produce and deploy a significant biological weapons arsenal during the 1980s.[34] Yet the BWC provides a good example of the multiple uses of treaties and agreements—not only to provide multilateral regimes but also to build norms that provide the basis for independent U.S. action. The BWC has helped to create a strong normative prohibition on the use of biological weapons, such that no leading member of the world community today publicly claims a right to maintain such an arsenal.[35] Along with similar agreements regarding weapons of mass destruction, the BWC has created a process of stigmatization and shaming for violators.[36] The United States has been able to employ these normative foundations to good effect in justifying and strengthening its responses to potential biological weapons attacks and violations.

The Chemical Weapons Convention has offered similar and even more fully institutionalized safeguards and enforcement mechanisms. It has also spawned related processes such as the Australia Group to help control the spread of chemical-weapons-related precursors. Like the BWC, it has a number of practical challenges—such as reliable verification and states meeting deadlines for the destruction of declared stocks[37]—but has also generated a similar norm by which the use of chemical weapons has become taboo in international relations.[38] The result has been a process with significant value to U.S. national interests.[39] The recent global response to the Syrian government's use of chemical weapons—and the subsequent U.S. condemnation and even-

---

[33] Monath and Gordon, 1998.

[34] Distinguishing illicit from responsible biological research is also extremely difficult in practice; the United States rejected a proposed biological weapons inspection protocol in 2001 in part out of concerns that it would allow foreign governments to interfere with U.S. corporations ("U.S. Rejection," 2001).

[35] Tarini, 2016; Isla, n.d.

[36] Shamat, 2015.

[37] Robinson, 1996.

[38] Price, 2007.

[39] Tucker, 2001.

tual removal of the remaining arsenal from Syria—helped to reinforce the norm, but it also demonstrated how the norm both justified U.S. actions and provided the means to strengthen them, in part by recruiting other states to the effort.[40]

This same model for conceiving the value of elements of order holds true in the nuclear realm, as partly described in the text box that follows. As late as the 1970s, many observers still feared a global surge of nuclear proliferation. The global nonproliferation regime created norms, offered a focal point for cooperation, and legitimized sanctions against violators.[41] The NPT is the most far-reaching of these agreements (both in scope and membership), and it serves as the foundation of the nuclear nonproliferation regime.

Some scholars take the view that the NPT is little more than a symbolic forum for states that independently decided to remain nonnuclear to signal their intentions to the rest of the world. The NPT, in this view, is not the cause but rather the effect of nonproliferation.[42] Yet the literature on the treaty points to a number of specific mechanisms by which it constrains proliferation. First, in being a near-universal global institution, it creates a strong presumption against proliferation in the vast majority of cases. The empirical record speaks to some degree of constraint: Only 9 countries to date have developed nuclear weapons, even though as many as 44 countries have the capacity to produce their own nuclear weapons systems.[43] Moreover, a handful of countries that did build their own bombs—South Africa, Belarus, Ukraine, and Kazakhstan—decided to destroy or surrender their weapons, reverting to a nonnuclear posture.[44]

---

[40] Edwards and Cacciatori, 2016.

[41] Ruggie, 1995, pp. 64–65.

[42] Betts, 1999, p. 62. Similarly, Jana von Stein notes that because membership in the NPT is voluntary, the treaty simply filters out states that have no intention of complying with it rather than constraining the behavior of the states that choose to become party to the treaty; put simply, the treaty "screens" rather than shapes state behavior (Von Stein, 2005, p. 612). See also Fuhrmann and Yonatan, 2016, p. 6.

[43] Rublee, 2009, p. 421.

[44] Sagan and Waltz, 2003, p. 182.

Case Study of Complementarity: Nuclear Nonproliferation

The issue area of preventing the spread of nuclear weapons provides an excellent example of how the three major categories of causal effect in the postwar order—U.S. power, the institutional and community-based effects of the international order, and broad trends in politics and economics—can work together in complementary ways to positive effect.

In the case of nuclear nonproliferation, U.S. power has served both to reassure and to deter. The U.S. extended deterrent umbrella over allies such as Germany and Japan has reduced the incentive to seek independent nuclear arsenals, while the threat of punishment has affected the cost-benefit calculations of states such as Libya and Syria. The spread of democracy brought governments to power in places such as Ukraine and South Africa, which saw less reason for nuclear arsenals.

But the combined effect of the order's various components has played an important role alongside these factors, and indeed those other variables might not have had the effect they did without the role of the order. It has offered institutions such as the NPT and IAEA to symbolize the global commitment to nuclear nonproliferation and to offer legitimate multilateral tools for the enforcement of agreements. Its normative component reflects powerful taboos on the use or, in most cases, acquisition of nuclear weapons. And the coalition of interest-sharing states at the core of the order has confronted would-be proliferators with expulsion from the shared international society and economy.

In cases ranging from Ukraine's post–Cold War surrender of former Soviet weapons to Libya's disarmament, we see the combined effect of these factors working together: strong multilateral diplomacy led by the officials of leading international organizations; pressure and diplomacy from many key members of the order's leading states; and U.S. pressure, reassurances, and threats, as needed, all deployed with the conscious justification of the order's broadly accepted norms.

The treaty has also promoted global nonproliferation norms, which helped to restrain the spread of nuclear weapons.[45] It has provided a forum for open communication and sharing of information;[46] established trust between actors through transparency, oversight, and repeated interactions;[47] mitigated uncertainty about other member states' intentions and capabilities;[48] and increased the costs of violating treaty obligations by establishing punitive measures for defections and holding states accountable to each other.[49] Taking these and other factors into account—and trying to disaggregate the effect of the NPT from other variables—an extensive empirical and qualitative, case-based literature has demonstrated that the treaty has had an effect in constraining weapons of mass destruction.[50] One study analyzed nuclear proliferation from 1970 to 2000 and concludes that "even after accounting for strategic selection into the treaty, NPT ratification is robustly associated with lower likelihoods of pursuing and obtaining nuclear weapons."[51]

Within the domestic sphere, moreover, laws, verification bodies, and interest groups have arisen to encourage and verify reductions in arms of all sorts in dozens of countries. This synergy between NPT membership and a country's domestic politics can "lock in" the state's nonnuclear posture.[52] A country's commitment to the NPT provides a basis for domestic political or special interests actors to pressure the

---

[45] See, for example, Coe and Vaynman, 2015; Fortna, 2003; N. Miller, 2014; Monteiro and Debs, 2014; and Nye, 1981. A more comprehensive study is Way and Sasikumar, 2004, pp. 32–33.

[46] Dai, 2012, p. 408.

[47] S. Mitchell and Hensel, 2007, p. 722.

[48] Meyer, 1984, p. 24.

[49] Dai, 2012, p. 412. This line of analysis stresses the importance of the IAEA in serving as a meaningful, shared verification system; see S. Mitchell and Hensel, 2007; Nye, 1981; Simmons and Hopkins, 2005; and N. Miller, 2014. See also Brown and Kaplow, 2014, p. 406.

[50] Fuhrmann and Yonatan, 2016.

[51] Fuhrmann and Yonatan, 2016, p. 3.

[52] Potter, 2010, p. 73.

government to maintain a nonnuclear posture, particularly when the aims of these actors overlap with those of the treaty.[53]

The NPT and associated institutions of the order, combined with strong U.S. pressure and the reassurance effect of U.S. alliance commitments, have contributed to a related and equally important objective: preventing the use of nuclear weapons. Partly this is through the emergence of a "nuclear taboo,"[54] a norm of nonuse that has emerged in concert with the NPT, become institutionalized in international conventions, and been strengthened by national policy and practice since 1945. These policies have included national no-first-use policies, as well as general policy statements rejecting the casual employment of nuclear weapons. The norms and institutions of the order have therefore contributed significantly to a critical U.S. goal in the post-1945 era—ensuring that no nuclear weapons are used in war.

Summary: The Security Value of the Order

Various elements of the postwar order have therefore been associated with a number of positive postwar trends, including the absence of major-power conflict and limits to the proliferation of weapons of mass destruction. Some of these benefits are very specific, with a direct and measurable causal connection—such as the role of the U.S. alliance system in deterring war. Others are more indirect, such as the creation of a predominant coalition devoted to the norm of nonaggression. Taken together, however, the available evidence suggests that the postwar order and U.S. military power have worked together to play a leading role in achieving gains in security.

---

[53] See, for example, Potter, 2010; Rublee, 2009; and Reiter, 2014.

[54] On the nuclear taboo, see Tannenwald, 2007.

CHAPTER SEVEN

Measuring Value: Normative Considerations and Value Promotion

The order's institutions, their included rules, and the broader norms they reflect work together to facilitate cooperation on shared issues. A multilateral order creates both more opportunities for cooperation and a shared expectation of collaborative problem solving, in part because it encourages a broad "sense of ownership" of the existing order. Specific elements of the order, such as treaties, create reliable commitments and thus facilitate ongoing cooperation.[1] Table 7.1 outlines ways in which the order has helped to establish norms and facilitate cooperation, again alongside and in concert with U.S. power and broad global trends.

This category of benefits of the order relies heavily on the persuasive role of norms and the systemic influence of status and prestige effects. The concept of stigma also illustrates this systemic effect. Once a dominant in-group is in place and the concern for status and prestige begins to influence thinking, stigmas, applied to behavior considered against the rules, can shape behavior over time.[2] Treaties can establish the basis for applying stigma to violators: More than most general state policies, treaties "are embedded in a broader system of socially

---

[1] As Simmons explains, research suggests that "treaties have made an important contribution to the ability of states to contract with one another: to make deals that are credible and follow rules that are relatively clear" (2010, p. 292).

[2] Adler-Nissen, 2014.

Table 7.1
Value of the International Order: Norms and Value Promotion

U.S. Objectives

- Promote human rights
- Promote and defend norms in key areas such as nonproliferation
- Advance prevalence of democracy

Contributing Factors

Leading Trends
- Rise of democracy creates basis for shared values and norms
- Global human rights progress in part through institutionalized norms

Role of U.S. Power
- U.S. value promotion helps promote and defend norms
- Direct assistance to democracies helps underwrite long-term trend
- Example of system offers goal for reforming countries

Elements of the Postwar Order
- Norms, institutions, and expectations of the order promote the rule of law
- Norms and institutions constrain international criminal activities
- Advancing transparency and anticorruption initiatives
- Promoting human rights through normative context created by conventions and treaties

Evidence for Effects of Order

- Empirical evidence of the effect of institutions in relevant normative areas
- Empirical evidence on long-term corruption and transparency trends
- Empirical and case-specific evidence for effect of human rights institutions
- Long-term trends in human rights norms

constructed inter-state rule making, normatively linked by . . . the idea that agreements of a legally obligatory nature must be observed."[3]

Promoting the Rule of Law

One central value of the international order has been the rule of law as a collective good.[4] The order's economic foundations depend on reliable rule of law in participating countries, so that general rules will be

---

[3] Simmons, 2010, p. 277; see also p. 292.

[4] An excellent resource that defines the rule of law in specific category terms and assesses its prospects around the world is World Justice Project, 2016.

respected and enforced within domestic contexts. These expectations extend to such issues as enforcement of contracts, protection of intellectual property, financial regulations, and more. As a result, the combined market at the core of the economic order has demanded effective rule of law, which has become established as a central norm. The United Nations has identified it as a critical norm of the order.[5]

The order's institutions have then actively promoted this norm in a number of ways. The leading one is conditionality—requiring certain reforms in order to gain membership to many of the order's defining components, such as military alliances or the WTO. Another mechanism of promoting the rule of law is through active capacity-building programs, which aim to build professional public- and private-sector institutions in member countries. The order's institutions have also built rule-of-law provisions into other activities, such as World Bank development programs and IMF loans. More broadly, the postwar economic order has created a context in which rule-of-law-oriented domestic reform has been viewed as useful and even necessary to achieve national prosperity.[6] Some empirical evidence suggests that such efforts, for example as part of the international trade regime, have bolstered the rule of law in China,[7] Singapore, and the Association of Southeast Asian Nations.[8]

Controlling International Criminal Activities

A second norm associated with the postwar order has been cooperation to combat international criminal enterprises and enforcement of shared standards on criminal activity. Transnational criminal activity is now

---

[5] United Nations, n.d.d. See also United Nations, 2008.

[6] As one study concluded, "The numerous international institutions present in the international system during the current economic crisis serve as conveyors of information and mechanisms of commitment and socialization. They mitigate the uncertainty problem that prevails in prisoner's dilemma settings such as trade. . . . The paper finds strong support for the role of international institutions as commitment and socialization mechanisms in preventing the rise of protectionism" (Baccini and Kim, 2012, p. 369).

[7] Li and Minyou, 2015; Hu, 2000; Hsu and Arner, 2007.

[8] Ewing-Chow, Losari, and Slade, 2014.

addressed through a thick international web of law enforcement and intelligence-sharing activities,[9] strongly institutionalized counterterrorism cooperation,[10] counterpiracy activities, and many more initiatives. The order has helped to strengthen the normative requirement to cooperate with such measures and underwritten the creation of more-elaborate and more-powerful international institutions to facilitate and coordinate that activity.

The Norm of Transparency and Anticorruption

Another major example is the area of rule-of-law and anticorruption initiatives.[11] One study found that the emergence of a global anticorruption norm had been "unusual for its breadth and rapid emergence."[12] Numerous anticorruption initiatives are under way under the aegis of the United Nations, the World Bank, the Organization for Economic Cooperation and Development, and other international institutions. Some reviews of the evidence find mixed results in terms of the ability of emerging social norms to directly affect corrupt practices,[13] but many studies find a measurable positive impact on domestic practices.[14] Another recent study examines international NGOs as policy entrepreneurs pushing anticorruption approaches globally.[15] One empirical study shows this effect in powerful terms: It found that international integration is strongly associated with reductions in corruption. It concludes that integration produces "economic and normative pressures" that raise the costs of corruption.[16]

---

[9]   On the role of institutions in particular, see Ristau, Zvekic, and Warlow, 1996.

[10]   Romaniuk, 2010.

[11]   See Heineman and Heimann, 2006; and Khaghaghordyan, 2014.

[12]   McCoy and Heckel, 2001, p. 66.

[13]   See Lindner, 2014.

[14]   C. Rose, 2015.

[15]   De Sousa, Larmour, and Hindess, 2009.

[16]   Sandholtz and Gray, 2003, p. 787.

Establishing and Advancing Human Rights

A fourth value is in the area of value promotion. Nine core international human rights conventions make up the international human rights regime, captured in Table 7.2. Many studies have turned up complex and mixed evidence about the direct relationship between human rights treaties and state behavior. As with many other international institutions, membership in human rights conventions is voluntary, and thus these treaties tend to attract states that already protect human rights or intend to improve their human rights track

Table 7.2
International Human Rights Regime

Convention	Date Created	Monitoring Body
International Convention on the Elimination of All Forms of Racial Discrimination	12/21/1965	Committee on the Elimination of All Forms of Racial Discrimination
International Covenant on Civil and Political Rights	12/16/1966	Committee on Civil and Political Rights
International Covenant on Economic, Social, and Cultural Rights	12/16/1966	Committee on Economic, Social, and Cultural Rights
Convention on the Elimination of All Forms of Discrimination Against Women	12/18/1979	Committee on the Elimination of All Forms of Discrimination Against Women
Convention Against Torture and Other Cruel, Inhuman, or Degrading Treatment or Punishment	12/10/1984	Committee Against Torture
Convention on the Rights of the Child	11/20/1989	Committee on the Rights of the Child
International Convention on the Protection of the Rights of All Migrant Workers and Members of Their Families	12/18/1990	Committee on Migrant Workers
Convention on the Rights of Persons with Disabilities	12/13/2006	Committee on the Rights of Persons with Disabilities
International Convention for the Protection of All Persons from Enforced Disappearance	12/20/2006	Committee on Enforced Disappearances

records.[17] The voluntary, self-selective nature of treaties often means that treaties may simply "screen" rather than constrain state behavior: States that sign them already respected their principles and did not have to make major alterations in their behavior.[18]

Yet it would be wrong to write off the positive influence of the massive postwar complex of human rights and democratization treaties, NGOs, conventions, and policies. While it may be difficult to trace the outcome of any one specific membership decision, there can be no question that the regime has paralleled an impressive global rise in democratic and liberal practices: Just about every global measure of freedom, from democratization to economic freedom, underwent a profound jump from the mid-1980s through the early 2000s, and this was not solely the result of the end of the Cold War.[19] The global emphasis on human rights in particular has undergone a revolution since 1945.[20] This correlation does not prove causation, but there are a number of proven avenues through which the international human rights order has affected state behavior.

First, it signals the value of joining human rights conventions. Ratification of such treaties can engage "audience costs" that create potential credibility problems for states that join and then disregard them. Many states join treaties with little regard for following their dictates—but in doing so, they have committed themselves to those principles, commitments that can become the basis for later pressure to meet them. Second, the international human rights regime engages domestic constituencies, laying the foundation for the development of NGOs dedicated to monitoring and improving human rights practices in countries with poor track records.[21] Third, international organiza-

---

[17] See, for instance, Cole, 2005; Chayes and Chayes, 1995; Goodliffe and Hawkins, 2006; and Hathaway, 2007.

[18] See Lupu, 2013; and Von Stein, 2005.

[19] Simmons, Dobbin, and Garrett, 2006, pp. 783–784.

[20] Iriye, Goedde, and Hitchcock, 2012.

[21] See Hafner-Burton, 2008; Murdie and Davis, 2012; and Dai, 2005. Simmons argues that some human rights treaties were "successful at improving human rights practices through agenda setting, litigation, and mobilization" (Simmons, 2009, p. 7). See also Simmons and Danner, 2010; and Kelley, 2007.

tions can work in tandem with conventions and treaties to promote human rights, in differing ways. Erik Voeten's work on the European Court of Human Rights argues that judges there have largely been independent of state influence and that the institution has thus had an important independent impact.[22]

Through the specific means just outlined, therefore, the postwar human rights regime has played an import role in giving institutional form to the aspirations for stronger human rights practices. It has served U.S. interests by establishing a stronger legal and normative baseline for the liberal values so central to U.S. foreign policy and the American national ethos.

Summary: The Normative Value of the Order

The postwar multilateral order has therefore played an important role in promoting the value-based outcomes that the United States has sought in world politics since 1945. Through institutions including conventions and treaties, the order has focused attention on normative issues, created benchmarks against which states are judged, and tied the prestige of countries to their standing on such indices. The order also boosted the case for such normative outcomes as the rule of law by conditioning membership in key institutions on progress in such areas. The order has thus supported a far stronger and more institutionalized form of the value promotion that has been central to U.S. foreign policy.

---

[22] Voeten, 2008. See also Burley and Mattli, 1993; and Helfer and Voeten, 2014. James Lebovic and Erik Voeten have argued that states can "launder" their human rights agendas through international organizations: They find strong statistical evidence for the proposition that critical resolutions at the UN Commission on Human Rights "for poor human rights performance are correlated with large reductions in World Bank and multilateral loan commitments," even though they have little effect on bilateral aid (Lebovic and Voeten, 2009, p. 93).

CHAPTER EIGHT

Estimating Measurable Benefits of the Order

Finally, we reviewed evidence for possible measurable value in ten sample issue areas. These appear in Table 8.1. In each case we offered a judgment, based on historical comparisons, of a potential counterfactual scenario absent the existence of such institutions, norms, and core community of states. We have used existing economic research to offer rough estimates of the potential cost represented by the counterfactual scenarios.

These counterfactual-based estimates are necessarily imprecise, in part because we cannot know for certain what economic or security events would have transpired in the absence of the elements of the postwar order. For each issue or event, we have identified relatively objective estimates for one phase of the analysis: the likely cost, in terms of economic activity or budgetary resources, of the counterfactual scenario. We know how much U.S. allies contributed to certain wars, for example; economists have estimated the possible cost of trade wars. (These values appear in the right-hand column of Table 8.1.) Our general research confirmed that elements of the postwar order did play some role in averting the negative outcomes reflected there, as either a necessary condition or a contributory variable. What this analysis cannot prove is the exact *proportion* of the resulting value that can be assigned to the order as opposed to other factors.

The postwar order therefore cannot be credited with preserving the sum total of the values listed in Table 8.1. Those are total outcomes *to which the elements of the order made important contributions* but that are the result of multiple factors. This analysis does point to possible

Table 8.1
Measurable Value of the Order

Issue/Event	Identifiable Role for Order: Institutions, Multilateralism, Role of Core States	Counterfactual Scenario	Value Associated with Difference: Total
Economic Affairs			
Sustaining postwar tariff reduction	The GATT process set in motion tariff reduction, which, even with the stagnation of recent WTO rounds, has been institutionalized as a global norm and avoided a reversion to high tariff rates.	Absent a multilateral trading order, tariff reductions would have been less likely; during economic crises, surges of tariff-imposing protectionism would have been highly likely.	2–5+ percent difference in GDP growth rate for multiple years; 300,000+ jobs[a]
2008 financial crisis: avoiding precipitous collapse	Numerous multilateral institutions engaged in extensive consultation and coordinated actions to dampen the effects of the financial contagion.[b]	Without the institutional basis for cooperation or the normative assumption of multilateral responses, several key elements of the response could have been absent.	Preserve economic activity equal to 5–10 percent of U.S. GDP, 4–6 million jobs; avoid budget deficit reaching 15–20 percent of GDP[c]
2008 crisis aftermath: avoiding trade war	G-20, the IMF, the Bank for International Settlements, and other institutions worked to reinforce habits of open trade and avoid large-scale protectionist responses. Various forms of protectionism have been growing since 2000, but a large-scale, 1930s-style trade war did not materialize.[d]	Absent both institutions and habits, states turn to a series of tariff wars and nontariff barriers from which states partially recover but that impose a significant short-term cost and leave countries less integrated.	Preserve economic activity ≥2–2.4 percent of world GDP growth and cut unemployment by ≥4 percent for 2+ years[e]

Table 8.1—Continued

Issue/Event	Identifiable Role for Order: Institutions, Multilateralism, Role of Core States	Counterfactual Scenario	Value Associated with Difference: Total
International standardization	Multiple international standard-setting bodies promulgate shared standards in areas ranging from telecommunications to consumer electronics to safety and quality. These multilateral processes generate positive economic externalities through enhanced efficiency, boosted trade, reduced training costs, and multiple other means.	In a world in which coordinated action collapses, joint international standard setting would be intermittent and very limited. Different regional blocs or countries would promulgate self-serving standards. The advantages of joint standards would be largely lost.	Various estimates of 15–40 percent productivity rise over various time horizons, 5–20 percent increase in output from all standards; or 1 percent increase in stock produces 0.05–0.12 percent increase in productivity[f]
Security Affairs			
Balkan crises	A coalition of states intervened to end civil war. European contributions of 90 percent of the financial costs and 80 percent of the peacekeeping troops in the Balkans (as of 2000, the EU had contributed $17 billion versus $5.5 billion for the United States) and provided over 75 percent of peacekeeping forces.[g]	Without the institutional basis for cooperation or the normative assumption of multilateral responses, the United States might have been forced to act alone or with a much smaller coalition, sharing fewer burdens.	$10–$15 billion in direct costs plus presence of 5,000 or more peacekeepers for 20 years[h]
Persian Gulf War	The United States operated under UN mandates for legitimacy and recruited a broad-ranging coalition to support the action and share the financial burden. Allies and friends provided over $45 billion in financial support.[i]	Without norms to justify action and a UN system to organize consensus, the action would have been far less legitimate. Friends would have seen less need to support the war.	$40+ billion plus significant effect on U.S. reputation and legitimacy[j]

Table 8.1—Continued

Issue/Event	Identifiable Role for Order: Institutions, Multilateralism, Role of Core States	Counterfactual Scenario	Value Associated with Difference: Total
Lost trade concessions	A RAND study sought to estimate the value of U.S. alliances in terms of improved trade treatment on the part of allies and partners.[k]	Absent the U.S. role in these alliances and partnerships, the states involved would have less reason to grant concessions on trade deals.	**$490 billion annual value to GDP**
Averting conflict in Taiwan and Korea	At multiple points, pressure from the order's norms, institutions, and core coalition of states has worked with U.S. military power and other factors to avert additional conflicts. This has been particularly notable in the cases of Taiwan (where Chinese aggression has been subordinated to a desire to play in the order) and Korea (where a UN command, bilateral alliance, and global normative order have helped to deter North Korean aggression).	In the absence of a multilateral order, both of these potential aggressors would have confronted far fewer constraints on action. A fragmented global system would have resulted in a smaller price for China to pay for grabbing Taiwan; the absence of a UN mandate, an alliance, or global nonaggression norms would change the context for North Korean calculations.	**$150 billion– $2+ trillion[l] if United States fought one war; risk of tens of billions of dollars in global economic costs from impact on markets even if it stood aloof**

Normative and Value Benefits

Counterpiracy initiatives	The collaboration on this issue reflects multilateral, informally institutionalized efforts. Levels of piracy dropped precipitously once cooperation, including associated naval operations and self-defense initiatives by shipping companies, began.	Absent institutions of maritime and national security coordination, the global response would have been far more ad hoc and less effective.[m]	**$18 billion in direct costs of piracy[n]**

Table 8.1—Continued

Issue/Event	Identifiable Role for Order: Institutions, Multilateralism, Role of Core States	Counterfactual Scenario	Value Associated with Difference: Total
Transparency and anticorruption	Institutions, gravitational, and coercive effect of coordinated markets produce emphasis on transparency and anticorruption initiatives. The actual amount of change as a result of order is difficult to measure but significant.	The absence of combined market and coordinated policies dampens pressure for transparency and reduced corruption. Fragmented order creates some poles of influence that embrace nepotistic and rent-seeking socioeconomic models.	Cost of corruption over $1.2 trillion for bribery effects alone, more in terms of lost productivity[o]

[a]There are many estimates of the potential cost of significant slides into protectionism, including tariffs, border taxes, and other mechanisms. The numbers cited here reflect a conservative estimate derived from sources such as Davies, 2017; Irwin, 2005; Krol, 2008; Ossa, 2011; and Tankersley 2016.

[b]For details on the IMF's responses, see Strauss-Kahn, 2009; and International Monetary Fund, 2016.

[c]A number of studies have assessed the differences made by the policy responses to the 2008 crisis; many focus on the discrete U.S. actions, though some include a discussion of international actions. The estimates here are compiled from these studies. See, for example, Drezner, *The System Worked*; Blinder and Zandi, 2015; Wheelock, 2010; and Porter, 2009. David Zaring points to the limitations of institutional responses in "Network and Treaty Performance during the Financial Crisis," (2009). More generally on the role of international economic coordination, see Eichengreen, 2011. Jonathan Kirschner compares the reaction to the Great Depression with the 2008 crisis, and while his emphasis is not on institutions or norms, many aspects of the "relatively benign" international environment he adduces as the difference—and the specific "monetary cooperation" he describes—fit the basic concept; see Kirschner, 2014.

[d]For an analysis of the limits to the post-crisis protectionist measures undertaken, as well as the potential cost of a trade war, see Bussière et al., 2010.

[e]On the theoretical value of institutions in constraining protectionist pressures, see Maggi, 1999; Maggi and Rodriguez-Clare, 1998; and Staiger and Tabellini, 1999. Studies that link international institutions explicitly to protectionist restraint after 2008 include Gawande, Hoekman, and Cui, 2015; and Eichengreen, 2016, who discusses specifically the role of central bank coordination to reduce the beggar-thy-neighbor effects of activist monetary policies. Other studies that examine the relationship between the crisis and trade include Shelburne, 2010; and UNCTAD, 2010, which concluded that "the recent crisis . . . has demonstrated that the multilateral trade rules under the World Trade Organization (WTO) worked effectively as a 'bulwark' against a wide-spread protectionism in the light of global recessionary concerns. Almost all trade policy measures that were introduced as a response to the financial crisis were consistent with the WTO rules" (p. xi).

Table 8.1—Continued

[f]For a Canadian country study, see Conference Board of Canada, 2007. A UK study on domestic standards is British Standards Institution, n.d. An Australian study is Standards Australia, n.d. These figures could be partially substituted with domestic standards that had similar effects on productivity, but the resulting ecosystem would be less efficient still impose relative economic costs.

[g]Daalder, 2000, pp. 166–167.

[h]On the general cost of peacekeeping, with a particular focus on the Balkan operations, from which these estimates of savings are derived, see Thornberry, 1998; A. Johnson and Glenny, 2011; and United Nations, n.d.d.

[i]U.S. General Accounting Office, 1991.

[j]Costs derived from U.S. General Accounting Office, 1991.

[k]Egel et al., 2016.

[l]Daggett, 2010. In constant FY 2011 dollars, the Korean conflict cost $341 billion, the Vietnam War $738 billion, and the Persian Gulf War $102 billion. The most recent estimates of the budgetary costs for the wars in Iraq and Afghanistan since 2001 (and through FY 2018) range from official Department of Defense estimates of over $750 billion each to a recent academic study that suggests a total price tag for Iraq plus Afghanistan of over $5.6 trillion; see Department of Defense, 2017, and Crawford, 2017.

[m]The initiatives undertaken since the mid-2000s include a mix of collective security efforts, such as coordinated naval deployments to the waters near Somalia, and actions by shipping companies to render their vessels more resilient to attack. It is the combination of these measures that achieved the reduction from 2010 to 2016. As in other issues, elements of a shared order cannot take complete credit for these values—but they were arguably a necessary condition for the achievements.

[n]The specific source for the $18 billion estimate is E. Greenberg, Hirt, and Smit, 2017. Related sources that spell out the role of international collaboration and the price of piracy include Besley, Fetzer, and Mueller, 2012; and Bowden, 2010.

[o]International Monetary Fund, 2016, pp. 5–14. See also World Bank, 2017.

measurable value for the order in two ways, however. First, it begins to give some sense of the significant value, in terms of economic growth, employment, and budgetary outlays that are associated with issues on which the order has had a definable impact. Second, in a number of these cases—notably, allied contributions to conflicts and the multilateral responses to recent economic and financial crises—elements of the order may well have been necessary (though not sufficient) factors in avoiding the counterfactual dangers posed here. In such cases, even given the role of other variables, the absence of a functioning multilateral order alone would have produced very significant costs, for the United States as well as the international community.

In the economic elements, our analysis attempted to measure two broad categories of effect. One is direct financial or other measurable economic contributions—areas such as allied financial support for U.S. military operations. In some cases these provide direct budgetary offsets for the United States. The other category is enhanced or preserved economic activity—most notably U.S. or global GDP growth and employment. In many cases these benefits derive from avoiding negative outcomes, such as trade wars and deeper recessions following financial crises. Our suggested value of the order in these cases stems from economic estimates of the possible consequences of such negative outcomes.

The challenge, as with all estimates of the order's value, is that it is difficult to distinguish variables associated with the order from other factors producing these benefits. For example, one refers to the cost-sharing contribution of U.S. allies and partners to the Persian Gulf War.[1] This was in part a product of the norms of multilateralism and nonaggression at stake in that conflict, and the institutional backing provided by the United Nations. But it was also a product of simple national interest calculations, especially by Gulf States, which would have been present to some degree with or without an overarching order.

There is no simple way to resolve this uncertainty. Our research suggests that elements of the order—institutions, norms, multilateral habits, the role of an implicit community of states at the core of the

---

[1]   Some would argue that the U.S. role in the Gulf War, as in many post-1945 U.S. commitments, reflects exclusively the costs of the order rather than its benefits. Such endeavors, it can be argued, were undertaken to defend the order's norms; without an order, they might not have been necessary. Again, however, for the purposes of this report, we take the consistent post-1945 U.S. grand strategy of deep engagement, and the resulting global military engagements and posture, as a given. A different grand strategy, such as isolationism, would have generated very different direct costs. Postwar U.S. administrations, however, have argued that the U.S. grand strategy should seek to create a larger context in which the United States is safer and U.S. interests more secure. That approach would have generated significant global commitments even without an accompanying order. The question is whether, having committed itself to such a strategy, the United States benefits from the rules, norms, and institutions of the order.

international system—are associated with these categories of benefit. In some cases they represent *necessary but not sufficient causes* of the outcomes. In orders, elements of order *offer partial causal explanations*. Any multiplier we might have employed to generate order-specific numbers would be somewhat arbitrary, and we have resisted the temptation to do so. Instead, we offer a total figure for each example, of which the postwar order can claim responsibility for some proportion of the total value.

These figures are therefore suggestive. But they give some clue as to the tens and perhaps hundreds of billions of dollars of value—directly to the United States—represented by the institutional, normative, and community-based elements of the order. If even *one* of these counterfactual scenarios were to emerge with a weakened order—from a dramatically worsened recession to a regional conflict to a trade war—the price would vastly overshadow the cost of the U.S. contribution to the order, ranging from UN dues to IMF contributions to perhaps some marginal delta in military expenditure tied to specific alliances. (In fact, there is a strong argument that the United States would have to *increase* its military budget in the absence of a multilateral order, as it lost the constraining and stabilizing factors previously outlined.)

Finally, to estimate a total value estimate for the postwar order, we gathered current data on U.S. expenditures relative to the order, noted in Table 8.2, to compare them to potential benefits. There are at least two categories of costs: direct costs of U.S. support payments to international institutions and processes; and indirect costs of the U.S. strategy of global engagement, which can be—but are not necessarily—related to the multilateral order.

Creating a formal "balance sheet" for the postwar order is fraught with risk. Apart from annual budgetary costs of U.S. support for multilateral organizations, all the estimates in Tables 8.1 and 8.2 are debatable. As we have stressed, the proportion of value accounted for by the order cannot be precisely determined. These figures intentionally exclude debates about the costs—or benefits—of overall U.S. trade policy, which some would view as crucial to understanding the true balance sheet of the postwar order.

Table 8.2
U.S. Annual Contributions to Elements of the International Order
(Most Recent Available Year)

Direct Support to Institutions of Order	
Total U.S. contributions to international organizations, including United Nations, the strictly administrative expenses of the NATO institutions, and the WTO (*UN regular and special activities total $3.3 billion[a] annually*)	$10.488 billion[b]
Total multilateral development bank contributions (World Bank, Asian Development Bank, Inter-American Development Bank, etc.)	$2.285 billion[c]
International Monetary Fund (*present-value estimates of annual costs of reserves placed on deposit with IMF; not an actual annual expenditure per se*)	$1.2 billion (*Congressional Budget Office estimate, per $60 billion in IMF quota amount*)[d]
Total direct cost of order	**$14 billion annually**
Support for U.S. Global Role Related to—but Distinct from—Order	
Economic and security-oriented foreign assistance	$42.4 billion[e]
U.S. foreign military presence (*vast differences in estimates, complex methodologies*)	$20.9 billion[f]
Increment of defense budget required for global presence (*many estimates, differing methodologies*)	$50 billion–$150+ billion
Increment of diplomatic budget required for global role (*few estimates, rough calculation*)	$3 billion[g]
Total costs of U.S. global role	**$116–216 billion+ annually**

[a] J. Greenberg, 2017.

[b] U.S. Department of State, n.d.

[c] Nelson, 2017.

[d] Congressional Budget Office, 2016.

[e] Bearak and Gamio, 2016.

[f] This is a Department of Defense estimate cited in Preble, 2013.

[g] This figure refers to diplomatic activities alone and compared FY 2016 with the FY 2018 administration budget request as a sample of what a reduction aligned to a smaller international role would look like. Actual savings could be marginally larger, but the total diplomatic engagement budget was only $15.6 billion in FY 2016, and given some minimum requirement, the savings could not likely exceed $5 billion annually. See U.S. Department of State, 2017

Nonetheless, in developing a broad finding relative to the balance sheet of the order, we draw three general conclusions from Tables 8.1 and 8.2. First, *the costs of the predominant U.S. global role dwarf those of the multilateral order itself.* Annual budgetary requirements for foreign aid and national security stem from U.S. grand strategic choices, not necessarily from its participation in a multilateral order. In theory the United States could scale back its military commitments and save an annual amount of money that represents a multiple of what it pays into the institutions of the multilateral order. Indeed, we find several areas in which the order's existence has actually depressed the amount the United States must pay to sustain that dominant global role—an effect that would presumably continue at lower U.S. levels of commitment.

Second, *preventing a single occurrence of either of the two major outcomes the order seeks to avoid—a global economic depression or a regional conflict—provides impressive return on investment for the order.* In terms of the price of the order's institutions themselves, preventing a single global financial crisis or Iraq-sized conflict, for example, would avoid costs that amount to between 30 and 60 times the annual U.S. outlays for the order.

Third, *even absent such extreme events, the persistent cost-benefit calculus of the multilateral order would appear to be favorable.* Adding the value of international contributions to operations and outcomes favored by the United States—such as Balkan peacekeeping, the Persian Gulf War, ongoing operations in Afghanistan, IMF stability funds, and much more—the United States buys a great deal of international commitment for its modest annual outlay. Some of these contributions would occur in any case, given the simple national interests involved. But the total value of these contributions has been a significant multiple of U.S. annual outlays for the institutions of the order, meaning that even if only a third or less of those contributions can be traced to the leverage of the order itself, the value equation is still favorable.

CHAPTER NINE

Looking Ahead: The Continuing and Prospective Value of the Order

The primary focus of the research and analysis underlying this study has been the postwar order's value to date—whether it has had measurably positive outcomes for U.S. interests over the last 70 years. We conclude that despite very real constraints on the role of institutions and norms, some mixed evidence on specific points, and some gaps in the data, the balance of evidence supports the finding that the postwar order has played an important role—alongside U.S. power and general global trends in economics and politics—in helping to safeguard U.S. interests and promote U.S. objectives. Based on this analysis, we judge that some version of the order can continue to offer such beneficial effects for the U.S. national security strategy going forward.

In the broadest sense, at a time of accelerating interdependence in areas ranging from environmental issues to digital economics, a multilateral order may have become a precondition for achieving individual national interests. This analysis does not suggest that it is *sufficient*—other factors, including U.S. leadership, are critical—but a working global order based on principles of equitable multilateralism may be a *necessary* condition for the achievement of essential U.S. national security interests in the 21st century.

The experience since 1945 suggests specific ways in which the institutions, norms, order, and global community associated with the postwar order can play an important role in dealing with a number of national priorities. We would highlight three categories of such functions. One is *providing stabilizing ballast at a time of rising tension and entropy in world politics*. Established elements of the order can provide reference points and expected rules of the road to work alongside U.S. and allied powers in keeping the international system from going too far off track. The elements of the order can play this role in a number of ways:

- Preserving a foundational base of effective international trade and economic institutions to preserve a sense of shared fate—and value—in an international order.
- Sustaining the military alliances, and reaffirming the consensus among the critical mass of states at the core of the order, that offer deterrence against aggression.
- Highlighting areas in which major countries, including China and the United States, continue to work together in useful ways.
- Creating a default path to Chinese influence through leadership of a shared rather than selfishly Sinocentric order.

A second category of continuing value of the order is in *providing coordination and cooperation mechanisms to address shared challenges*. This is a classic function of institutions and remains highly relevant today. By far the most significant such shared challenge is climate change, which threatens the health of the ecosystem on which all human life depends. Already the multilateral processes and habits inherent in a shared order have begun to produce agreements on goals and initial steps, through the negotiations and commitments of such joint efforts as the Kyoto Protocol and the Paris Accord on climate. This process must deepen—and the U.S. leadership role must become far more decisive—if the multilateral order is to make the contribution required. From the standpoint of this analysis of the order's value, the critical point is that the institutions, norms, rules, and habits of the shared order built since 1945 offer a sound structural basis for such collaboration, one that offers the hope of far more effective action than would be possible without the components of the postwar order.

Beyond that leading issue, the order can be useful in promoting collaboration on a number of other issues, including

- the role of the United Nations Security Council in ratifying the attitude of global powers on such issues as North Korean nuclear violations
- offering mechanisms to coordinate activities to combat terrorism, radicalization, piracy, international crime, and more
- encouraging continued efforts to coordinate global standards on emerging issues such as cyber attacks and artificial intelligence.

Third and finally, the elements of the postwar order can *continue to build on the gradual socialization process under way since 1945.* The order has helped to establish certain cooperative processes, expectations, and norms that, while always subject and secondary to state interests, nonetheless have influenced both popular and official beliefs and actions. Going forward, these can include

- continued international support for a principle of nonaggression designed to preserve the trend of declining interstate conflict
- deepening networks of nonstate actors that link together members of the order and provide domestic support for key norms, such as human rights and good governance.

In sum, the collaborative mechanisms, implicit sense of global community, institutions, rules, norms, and habits that have accumulated since 1945 could potentially play an important role, and may in some cases be necessary, to meeting all of the major economic and security challenges that lie ahead. U.S. responses to these challenges—while continuing to demand both U.S. leadership and U.S. power—will be stronger and more effective if they are nested in the supportive context of a shared order. This is not to suggest that the components of that order can achieve outcomes on their own; as noted at the beginning of this analysis, we presume that the order has been effective to the degree that its role has merged with that of U.S. power and broader trends.

We find this conclusion to be especially persuasive given the alternatives that exist to a shared order for providing the basic framework for the U.S. grand strategy. A highly unilateralist, nationalist approach would risk undermining cooperation on key security issues and doing serious damage to the global economy. A retreat into a Cold War–style division of world politics designed to deter presumed revisionists would exacerbate risks of war—and is probably not feasible if China is the leading target of such an approach. This analysis therefore concludes that an imperfect but meaningful shared order with the United States at its hub remains the best available ordering mechanism to achieve both short- and long-term U.S. objectives.

References

Abbott, Frederick M., "NAFTA and the Legalization of World Politics: A Case Study," *International Organization*, Vol. 54, No. 3, Summer 2000, pp. 519–547.

Abbott, Kenneth W., Jessica F. Green, and Robert O. Keohane, "Organizational Ecology and Institutional Change in Global Governance," *International Organization*, Vol. 70, No. 2, 2016, pp. 247–277.

Abrego, Lisandro, and Carlo Perroni, "Free-Riding, Carbon Treaties, and Trade Wars: The Role of Domestic Environmental Policies," *Journal of Development Economics*, Vol. 58, 1999, pp. 463–483.

Adler-Nissen, Rebecca, "Stigma Management in International Relations: Transgressive Identities, Norms, and Order in International Society," *International Organization*, Vol. 68, Winter 2014, pp. 143–176.

Affolder, Natasha A., "The Private Life of Environmental Treaties," *American Journal of International Law*, Vol. 103, No. 3, July 2009, pp. 510–525. As of January 12, 2017:
http://www.jstor.org/stable/40283654

Aldy, Joseph E., and Robert N. Stavins, *Architectures for Agreement: Addressing Global Climate Change in the Post-Kyoto World*, Cambridge: Cambridge University Press, 2007.

Allee, Todd L., and Jamie E. Scalera, "The Divergent Effects of Joining International Organizations: Trade Gains and the Rigors of WTO Accession," *International Organization*, Vol. 66, No. 2, 2012, pp. 243–276.

Almer, Christian, and Ralph Winkler, "Analyzing the Effectiveness of International Environmental Policies: The Case of the Kyoto Protocol," *Journal of Environmental Economics and Management*, Vol. 82, November 2016, pp. 125–151. As of January 12, 2017:
http://dx.doi.org/10.1016/j.jeem.2016.11.003

Anderson, Christopher J., "When in Doubt, Use Proxies: Attitudes Toward Domestic Politics and Support for European Integration," *Comparative Political Studies*, Vol. 31, No. 5, 1998, pp. 569–601.

Andrews, Edmund L., "IMF Loan to Brazil Also Shields U.S. Interests," *New York Times*, August 9, 2002.

Angelo, Mary Jane, Rebecca Bratspies, David Hunter, John H. Knox, Noah Sachs, and Sandra Zellmer, *Reclaiming Global Environmental Leadership: Why the United States Should Ratify Ten Pending Environmental Treaties*, Center for Progressive Reform, White Paper #1202, January 2012. As of January 12, 2017: http://www.progressivereform.org/articles/ international_environmental_treaties_1201.pdf

Ansley, Rachel, "Making the Case for Multilateralism," *The Atlantic Council*, April 24, 2017.

Anthony, Ian, Camille Grand, Lukasz Kulesa, Christian Mölling, and Mark Smith, *Nuclear Weapons After the 2010 NPT Review Conference*, Chaillot Papers Series, Paris: European Union Institute for Security Studies, April 2010.

Arnold, Patricia J., "Institutional Perspectives on the Internationalization of Accounting," in Christopher S. Chapman, David J. Cooper, and Peter B. Miller, eds., *Accounting, Organizations, and Institutions*, New York: Oxford University Press, 2009, pp. 48–64.

Augier, P., M. Gasiorek, and C. L. Tong, "The Impact of Rules of Origin on Trade Flows," *Economic Policy*, Vol. 20, No. 43, 2005, pp. 568–624.

Axelrod, Robert, and Robert Keohane, "Achieving Cooperation Under Anarchy: Strategies and Institutions," *World Politics*, Vol. 38, No. 1, 1985, pp. 226–254.

Baccini, Leonardo, and Soo Yeon Kim, "Preventing Protectionism: International Institutions and Trade Policy," *Review of International Organizations*, Vol. 7, No. 4, 2012, pp. 369–398.

Bakker, Age, *International Financial Institutions*, New York: Longman; Heerlen: Open University of the Netherlands, 1996.

Baldwin, Richard E., "Multilateralising Regionalism: Spaghetti Bowls as Building Blocs on the Path to Global Free Trade," *The World Economy*, Vol. 29, No. 11, 2006, pp. 1451–1518.

———, "The World Trade Organization and the Future of Multilateralism," *Journal of Economic Perspectives*, Vol. 30, No. 1, Winter 2016, pp. 95–116.

Barro, Robert J., and Jong-wha Lee, "IMF Programs: Who Are Chosen and What Are the Effects?," unpublished paper, April 2003. As of November 14, 2017: https://openresearch-repository.anu.edu.au/bitstream/1885/40130/3/ wp-econ-2003-09.pdf

Bearak, Max, and Lazaro Gamio, "The U.S. Foreign Aid Budget, Visualized," *Washington Post*, October 18, 2016.

Bearce, David H., and Stacy Bondanella, "Intergovernmental Organizations, Socialization, and Member-State Interest Convergence," *International Organization*, Vol. 61, No. 4, 2007, pp. 703–733.

Beardsley, Kyle, "Peacekeeping and the Contagion of Armed Conflict," *Journal of Politics*, Vol. 73, No. 4, 2011, pp. 1051–1064.

———, "UN Intervention and the Duration of International Crises," *Journal of Peace Research*, Vol. 49, No. 2, 2012, pp. 335–349.

Beckley, Michael, "The Myth of Entangling Alliances: Reassessing the Security Risks of U.S. Defense Pacts," *International Security*, Vol. 39, No. 4, Spring 2015, pp. 7–48.

Beeson, Mark, and Stephen Bell, "The G-20 and International Economic Governance: Hegemony, Collectivism, or Both?," *Global Governance*, Vol. 15, No. 1, 2009, pp. 67–86. As of January 26, 2017: http://www.jstor.org/stable/27800739

Bensahel, Nora, "International Alliances and Military Effectiveness: Fighting Alongside Allies and Partners," in Risa A. Brooks and Elizabeth A. Stanley, eds., *Creating Military Power: The Sources of Military Effectiveness*, Stanford, Calif.: Stanford University Press, 2007, pp. 186–206.

Besley, Tim, Thiemo Fetzer, and Hannes Mueller, "The Economic Costs of Piracy," International Growth Centre, Policy Brief, April 2012.

Betts, Richard K., "Universal Deterrence or Conceptual Collapse? Liberal Pessimism and Utopian Realism," in Victor A. Utgoff, ed., *The Coming Crisis: Nuclear Proliferation, U.S. Interests, and World Order*, Cambridge, Mass.: MIT Press, 1999, pp. 51–85.

———, "Institutional Imperialism," *National Interest*, June 2011.

———, "Strong Arguments, Weak Evidence," *Security Studies*, Vol. 21, 2012, pp. 345–351.

Bhagwati, Jagdish, "Regionalism versus Multilateralism," *The World Economy*, Vol. 15, No. 5, 1992, pp. 535–556.

Bhargava, Vinay, "The Role of the International Financial Institutions in Addressing Global Issues," in *Global Issues for Global Citizens: An Introduction to Key Development Challenges*, Washington, D.C.: World Bank, 2006, pp. 393–409.

———, *Termites in the Trading System: How Preferential Agreements Undermine Free Trade*, New York: Oxford University Press, 2008.

Bird, Graham, "IMF Programs: Do They Work? Can They Be Made to Work Better?," *World Development*, Vol. 29, No. 11, 2001, pp. 1849–1865.

Bleek, Philipp, "Why Do States Proliferate? Quantitative Analysis of the Exploration, Pursuit, and Acquisition of Nuclear Weapons," in William C. Potter and Gaukar Makhatzhanova, eds., *Forecasting Nuclear Proliferation in the 21st Century: The Role of Theory*, Stanford, Calif.: Stanford University Press, 2010, pp. 159–192.

Bleek, Philipp C., and Eric B. Lorber, "Security Guarantees and Allied Nuclear Proliferation," *Journal of Conflict Resolution*, Vol. 58, No. 2, 2014, pp. 429–454.

Blinder, Alan S., and Mark Zandi, "The Financial Crisis: Lessons for the Next One," Center on Budget and Policy Priorities, October 15, 2015.

Blustein, Paul, *The Misadventures of the Most Favored Nations*, New York: PublicAffairs, 2009.

———, "The Inefficiency of International Financial Institutions," *Globe and Mail*, November 12, 2012.

Boehmer, Charles, Erik Gartzke, and Timothy Nordstrom, "Do Intergovernmental Organizations Promote Peace?," *World Politics*, Vol. 57, No. 1, 2004, pp. 1–38.

Böhmelt, Tobias, and Ulrich H. Pilster, "International Environmental Regimes: Legalisation, Flexibility and Effectiveness," *Australian Journal of Political Science*, Vol. 45, No. 2, 2010, pp. 245–260.

Boswell, Nancy Zucker, "Combating Corruption: Are International Institutions Doing Their Job?," *Proceedings of the ASIL Annual Meeting* (American Society of International Law), Vol. 90, March 1996, pp. 98–105.

Bowden, Anna, "The Economic Cost of Maritime Piracy," One Earth Future Working Paper, December 2010. As of November 20, 2017: http://oceansbeyondpiracy.org/sites/default/files/attachments/ The%20Economic%20Cost%20of%20Piracy%20Full%20Report.pdf

Bown, Chad P., "On the Economic Success of GATT/WTO Dispute Settlement," *Review of Economics and Statistics*, Vol. 86, No. 3, 2004, pp. 811–823.

Bown, Chad P., and Meredith A. Crowley, "Self-Enforcing Trade Agreements: Evidence from Time-Varying Trade Policy," *American Economic Review*, Vol. 103, No. 2, 2013, pp. 1071–1090.

Boyce, R., *The Great Interwar Crisis and the Collapse of Globalization*, Basingstoke, U.K.: Palgrave Macmillan, 2009.

Bratberg, Espe, Sigve Tjotta, and Torgeir Oines, "Do Voluntary International Environmental Agreements Work?," *Journal of Environmental Economics and Management*, Vol. 50, June 2005, pp. 583–597. As of January 12, 2017: http://dx.doi.org/10.1016/j.jeem.2005.03.002

Breitmeier, Helmut, Arild Underdal, and Oran R. Young, "The Effectiveness of International Environmental Regimes: Comparing and Contrasting Findings from Quantitative Research," *International Studies Review*, Vol. 13, No. 4, December 2011, pp. 579–605. As of January 12, 2017: http://www.jstor.org/stable/41428859

British Standards Institution, "Economic Benefits of Standards: Research Reports," n.d. As of November 9, 2017: https://www.bsigroup.com/en-GB/standards/benefits-of-using-standards/ research-reports/

Brooks, Stephen G., "The Globalization of Production and the Changing Benefits of Conquest," *Journal of Conflict Resolution*, Vol. 43, No. 5, October 1999, pp. 646–670.

Brooks, Stephen G., and William C. Wohlforth, *America Abroad: The United States' Global Role in the 21st Century*, New York: Oxford University Press, 2016.

Brown, Robert L., and Jeffrey M. Kaplow, "Talking Peace, Making Weapons: IAEA Technical Cooperation and Nuclear Proliferation," *Journal of Conflict Resolution*, Vol. 58, No. 2, 2014, pp. 402–428.

Brunee, Jutta, "The United States and International Environmental Law: Living with an Elephant," *European Journal of International Law*, Vol. 15, No. 4, 2004, pp. 617–649. As of January 12, 2017:
http://www.ejil.org/pdfs/15/4/373.pdf

Brysk, Alison, "Global Good Samaritans? Human Rights Foreign Policy in Costa Rica," *Global Governance*, Vol. 11, No. 4, 2005, pp. 445–466. As of November 9, 2017:
http://www.jstor.org/stable/27800585

Brysk, Alison, and William C. Wohlforth, *America Abroad: The United States' Global Role in the 21st Century*, New York: Oxford University Press, 2016.

Burley, Anne-Marie, and Walter Mattli, "Europe Before the Court: A Political Theory of Legal Integration," *International Organization*, Vol. 47, No. 1, Winter 1993, pp. 41–76.

Burton, David, "Asia and the International Monetary Fund: Ten Years After the Asian Crisis," in Bhumika Muchhala, ed., *Ten Years After: Revisiting the Asian Financial Crisis*, Washington, D.C.: Woodrow Wilson Center, October 2007, pp. 63–72.

Busch, Marc L., "Overlapping Institutions, Forum Shopping, and Dispute Settlement in International Trade," *International Organization*, Vol. 61, No. 4, 2007, pp. 735–761.

Busch, Marc L., and E. Reinhardt, "Developing Countries and General Agreement on Tariffs and Trade/World Trade Organization Dispute Settlement," *Journal of World Trade*, Vol. 37, No. 4, 2003, pp. 719–736.

Bush, Richard C., *In Support of U.S. Alliances*, Washington, D.C.: The Brookings Institution, September 29, 2016. As of November 9, 2017:
https://www.brookings.edu/research/in-support-of-u-s-alliances/

Bussière, Matthieu, Emilia Pérez-Barreiro, Roland Straub, and Daria Taglioni, *Protectionist Responses to the Crisis: Global Trends and Implications*, Occasional Paper Series No. 110, Frankfurt am Main: European Central Bank, May 2010.

Buzan, Barry, "From International System to International Society: Structural Realism and Regime Theory Meet the English School," *International Organization*, Vol. 47, No. 3, 1993, pp. 327–352.

Cairncross, Frances, "What Makes Environmental Treaties Work?," *Conservation Magazine*, July 29, 2008. As of January 12, 2017:
http://www.conservationmagazine.org/2008/07/
what-makes-environmental-treaties-work/

Campbell, Kurt M., Robert J. Einhorn, and Mitchell B. Reiss, eds., *The Nuclear Tipping Point: Why States Reconsider Their Nuclear Choices*, Washington, D.C.: Brookings Institution Press, 2004.

Camp Keith, Linda, "The United Nations International Covenant on Civil and Political Rights: Does It Make a Difference in Human Rights Behavior?," *Journal of Peace Research*, Vol. 36, 1999, pp. 95–118.

———, "Judicial Independence and Human Rights Protection around the World," *Judicature*, Vol. 85, No. 4, 2002, 195–201.

Cao, V. T., and L. Flach, "The Effect of GATT/WTO on Export and Import Price Volatility," *The World Economy*, Vol. 38, No. 12, December 2015, pp. 2049–2079.

Carey, Sabine C., Mark Gibney, and Steven C. Poe, *The Politics of Human Rights*, New York: Cambridge University Press, 2010.

Chafetz, Glenn, "The Political Psychology of the Nuclear Nonproliferation Regime," *Journal of Politics*, Vol. 57, No. 3, 1995, pp. 743–775.

Chase, K. A., *Trading Blocs: States, Firms, and Regions in the World Economy*, Ann Arbor: University of Michigan Press, 2005.

Chayes, Abram, and Antonia Chayes, *The New Sovereignty: Compliance with International Regulatory Agreements*, Cambridge, Mass.: Harvard University Press, 1995.

Chayes, Antonia, "How American Treaty Behavior Threatens National Security," *International Security*, Vol. 33, No. 1, Summer 2008, pp. 45–81. As of January 12, 2017:
http://www.jstor.org/stable/40207101

Checkel, Jeffrey T., "International Institutions and Socialization in Europe: Introduction and Framework," *International Organization*, Vol. 59, No. 4, 2005, pp. 801–826.

Cheibub, José, Jennifer Gandhi, and James Vreeland, "Democracy and Dictatorship Revisited," *Public Choice*, Vol. 143, 2010, pp. 67–101.

Chorev, Nitsan, and Sarah Babb, "The Crisis of Neoliberalism and the Future of International Institutions: A Comparison of the IMF and the WTO," *Theory and Society*, Vol. 38, No. 5, 2009, pp. 459–484. As of January 26, 2017:
http://www.jstor.org/stable/40345665

Cingranelli, David, and David Richards, "The Cingranelli and Richards (CIRI) Human Rights Data Project," *Human Rights Quarterly*, Vol. 32, 2010, pp. 395–418.

Claessens, Stijn, Ayhan Kose, Luc Laeven, and Fabian Valencia, "Financial Crises: Causes, Consequences, and Policy Responses," International Monetary Fund, February 19, 2014. As of January 26, 2017: https://www.imf.org/external/pubs/cat/longres.aspx?sk=40301.0

Clark, Rob, "A Tale of Two Trends: Democracy and Human Rights, 1981–2010," *Journal of Human Rights*, Vol. 13, No. 4, 2014, pp. 395–413.

Clemens, Michael A., and Jeffrey G. Williamson, "Why Did the Tariff-Growth Correlation Change After 1950?," *Journal of Economic Growth*, Vol. 9, No. 1, 2004, pp. 5–46.

Coe, Andrew, and Jane Vaynman, "Collusion and the Nuclear Nonproliferation Treaty," *Journal of Politics*, Vol. 77, No. 4, 2015, pp. 983–997.

Cole, Wade M., "Sovereignty Relinquished? Explaining Commitment to the International Human Rights Covenants, 1966–1999," *American Sociological Review*, Vol. 70, 2005, pp. 472–495.

———, "Hard and Soft Commitments to Human Rights Treaties, 1966–2000," *Sociological Forum*, Vol. 24, 2009, pp. 563–588.

———, "Human Rights as Myth and Ceremony? Reevaluating the Effectiveness of Human Rights Treaties, 1981–2007," *American Journal of Sociology*, Vol. 117, No. 4, 2012, pp. 1131–1171.

Conference Board of Canada, *Economic Value of Standardization*, Ottawa: Standards Council of Canada, July 2007.

Congressional Budget Office, "The Budgetary Effects of the United States' Participation in the International Monetary Fund," June 2016.

Conrad, Courtenay, "Divergent Incentives for Dictators: Domestic Institutions and (International Promises Not to) Torture," *Journal of Conflict Resolution*, Vol. 58, No. 1, 2014, pp. 34–67.

Conrad, Courtenay, and Emily Ritter, "Treaties, Tenure, and Torture: The Conflicting Domestic Effects of International Law," *Journal of Politics*, Vol. 75, No. 2, 2013, 397–409.

Copelovitch, Mark, *The International Monetary Fund in the Global Economy: Banks, Bonds, and Bailouts.* New York: Cambridge University Press, 2010.

Cortell, Andrew P., and James W. Davis, Jr., "How Do International Institutions Matter? The Domestic Impact of International Rules and Norms," *International Studies Quarterly*, Vol. 40, No. 4, 1996, pp. 451–478.

———, "When Norms Clash: International Norms, Domestic Practices, and Japan's Internalisation of the GATT/WTO," *Review of International Studies*, Vol. 31, No. 1, 2005, pp. 3–25.

Crawford, Neta C., "United States Budgetary Costs of Post-9/11 Wars through FY2018," Watson Institute of International and Public Affairs, Brown University, November 2017. As of November 20, 2017:
http://watson.brown.edu/costsofwar/files/cow/imce/papers/2017/Costs%20of%20U.S.%20Post=9_11%20NC%20Crawford%20FINAL%20.pdf

Daalder, Ivo, "The United States in the Balkans: There to Stay," *Washington Quarterly*, Vol. 23, No. 4, Autumn 2000, pp. 155–170.

Daggett, Stephen, "Costs of Major U.S. Wars," Congressional Research Service, June 29, 2010.

Dai, Xinyuan, "Why Comply? The Domestic Constituency Mechanism," *International Organization*, Vol. 59, No. 2, 2005, pp. 363–398.

———, "Information Systems in Treaty Regimes," *World Politics*, Vol. 54, No. 4, 2012, pp. 405–436.

———, "The Conditional Effects of International Human Rights Institutions," *Human Rights Quarterly*, Vol. 36, No. 3, 2014, pp. 569–589.

Danaher, Kevin, ed., *50 Years Is Enough: The Case Against the World Bank and the International Monetary Fund*, Boston: South End Press, 1994.

Dancy, Geoff, and Kathryn Sikkink, "Ratification and Human Rights Prosecutions: Toward a Transnational Theory of Treaty Compliance," *International Law and Politics*, Vol. 44, 2012, pp. 751–790.

Danilovic, Vesna, "The Sources of Threat Credibility in Extended Deterrence," *Journal of Conflict Resolution*, Vol. 45, No. 3, 2001, pp. 341–369.

Davies, Gavyn, "The Worrying Macro-Economics of U.S. Border Taxes," Fulcrum Asset Management LLP, January 1, 2017.

Davis, Christina L., and Meredith Wilf, "WTO Membership," in Lisa L. Martin, ed., *The Oxford Handbook of the Political Economy of International Trade*, New York: Oxford University Press, 2015, pp. 380–399.

De Sousa, Luis, Peter Larmour, and Barry Hindess, *Governments, NGOs and Anti-Corruption: The New Integrity Warriors*, London: Routledge, 2009.

Dorussen, Han, and Hugh Ward, "Intergovernmental Organizations and the Kantian Peace: A Network Perspective," *Journal of Conflict Resolution*, Vol. 52, No. 2, April 2008, pp. 189–212.

Downs, George W., David M. Rocke, and Peter N. Barsoom, "Is the Good News About Compliance Good News About Cooperation?," *International Organization*, Vol. 50, No. 3, 1996, pp. 379–406.

Doyle, Michael W., "A Liberal View: Preserving and Expanding the Liberal Pacific Union," in T. V. Paul and John Hall, eds., *International Order and the Future of World Politics*, Cambridge: Cambridge University Press, 1999, pp. 41–66.

Doyle, Michael W., and Nicholas Sambanis, "International Peacebuilding: A Theoretical and Quantitative Analysis," *American Political Science Review*, Vol. 94, No. 4, 2000, pp. 779–801.

———, *Making War and Building Peace: United Nations Peace Operations*, Princeton, N.J.: Princeton University Press, 2006.

Drezner, Daniel, *The System Worked: How the World Stopped Another Great Depression*, New York: Oxford University Press, 2016.

Duffield, John S., "International Regimes and Alliance Behavior: Explaining NATO Conventional Force Levels," *International Organization*, Vol. 46, No. 4, Fall 1992, pp. 819–855.

———, "Explaining the Long Peace in Europe: The Contributions of Regional Security Regimes," *Review of International Studies*, Vol. 20, No. 4, October 1994, pp. 369–388.

Easterly, William, *The Elusive Quest for Growth*, Cambridge, Mass.: MIT Press, 2001.

Edwards, Brett, and Mattia Cacciatori, "Syria and the Future of the Chemical Weapons Taboo," *E-International Relations*, March 21, 2016. As of November 9, 2017:
http://www.e-ir.info/2016/03/21/
syria-and-the-future-of-the-chemical-weapon-taboo/

Egel, Daniel, Adam Grissom, John P. Godges, Jennifer Kavanaugh, and Howard Shatz, *Estimating the Value of Overseas Security Commitments*, Santa Monica, Calif.: RAND Corporation, 2016.

Eichengreen, Barry, "International Financial Regulation After the Crisis," *Daedalus*, Vol. 139, No. 4, 2010, pp. 107–114. As of January 26, 2017:
http://www.jstor.org/stable/25790430

———, "International Policy Coordination: The Long View," unpublished paper, September 2011. As of December 3, 2017:
https://eml.berkeley.edu/~eichengr/intl_policy_coord_9-19-11.pdf

———, "The Great Depression in a Modern Mirror," *De Economist*, Vol. 164, No. 1, March 2016.

Eichengreen, Barry, and D. A. Irwin, "Trade Blocs, Currency Blocs and the Reorientation of World Trade in the 1930s," *Journal of International Economics*, Vol. 38, No. 1, 1995, pp. 1–24.

Eichengreen, Barry, and Kevin O'Rourke, "A Tale of Two Depressions," VoxEU.org, March 8, 2010. As of November 14, 2017:
http://voxeu.org/article/tale-two-depressions-what-do-
new-data-tell-us-february-2010-update

———, "A Tale of Two Depressions Redux," VoxEU.org, March 6, 2012. As of November 14, 2017:
http://voxeu.org/article/tale-two-depressions-redux

Elkins, Zachary, Andrew T. Guzman, and Beth A. Simmons, "Competing for Capital: The Diffusion of Bilateral Investment Treaties, 1960–2000," *International Organization*, Vol. 60, No. 4, October 2006, pp. 811–846.

Ellis, H. S., *Exchange Control in Central Europe*, Cambridge, Mass.: Harvard University Press, 1941.

Elrod, Richard B., "The Concert of Europe: A Fresh Look at an International System," *World Politics*, Vol. 28, No. 2, January 1976, pp. 159–174.

Englehart, Neil A., and Melissa K. Miller, "The CEDAW Effect: International Law's Impact on Women's Rights," *International Organization*, Vol. 13, 2014, pp. 22–47.

Erasmus, H., F. Flatters, and R. Kirk, "Rules of Origin as Tools of Development? Some Lessons from SADC," in Olivier Cadot, Antoni Estavadeoral, Akiko Suwa Eisenmann, and Thierry Verdier, eds., *The Origin of Goods: Rules of Origin in Regional Trade Agreements*, Oxford: Oxford University Press, 2006, pp. 259–294.

Ewing-Chow, Michael, Junianto James Losari, and Melania Vilarasau Slade, "The Facilitation of Trade by the Rule of Law: The Cases of Singapore and ASEAN," in Marion Jansen, Mustapha Sadni Jallab, and Maarten Smeets, eds., *Connecting to Global Markets*, Geneva: World Trade Organization, 2014, pp. 129–146. As of November 14, 2017:
https://www.wto.org/english/res_e/booksp_e/cmark_chap9_e.pdf

Falkner, Robert, "American Hegemony and the Global Environment," *International Studies Review*, Vol. 7, No. 4, December 2005, pp. 585–599. As of January 12, 2017:
http://www.jstor.org/stable/3699676

Fang, Songying, Jesse C. Johnson, and Brett Ashley Leeds, "To Concede or to Resist? The Restraining Effect of Military Alliances," *International Organization*, Vol. 68, Fall 2014, pp. 775–809.

Fariss, Christopher J., "Respect for Human Rights Has Improved over Time: Modeling the Changing Standard of Accountability in Human Rights Documents," *American Political Science Review*, Vol. 108, No. 2, 2014, pp. 297–318.

———, "The Changing Standard of Accountability and the Positive Relationship Between Human Rights Treaty Ratification and Compliance," *British Journal of Political Science*, 2017, pp. 1–33.

Finnemore, Martha, "International Organizations as Teachers of Norms: The United Nations Educational, Scientific, and Cultural Organization and Science Policy," *International Organization*, Vol. 47, No. 4, November 1993, pp. 565–597.

Florini, Ann, "The Evolution of International Norms," *International Studies Quarterly*, Vol. 40, No. 3, September 1996, pp. 363–389.

Foot, Rosemary S., Neil MacFarlane, and Michael Mastanduno, eds., *U.S. Hegemony and International Organizations: The United States and Multilateral Institutions*, Oxford: Oxford University Press, 2003.

Fortna, Virginia Page, "Scraps of Paper? Agreements and the Durability of Peace," *International Organization*, Vol. 57, No. 2, 2003, pp. 337–372.

———, "Does Peacekeeping Keep Peace? International Intervention and the Duration of Peace After Civil War," *International Studies Quarterly*, Vol. 48, 2004a, pp. 269–292.

———, "Interstate Peacekeeping: Causal Mechanisms and Empirical Effects," *World Politics*, Vol. 56, No. 4, 2004b, pp. 481–519.

Fortna, Virginia Page, and Lisa L. Martin, "Peacekeepers as Signals: The Demand for International Peacekeeping in Civil Wars," in Helen V. Milner, ed., *Power, Interdependence and Non-State Actors in World Politics: Research Frontiers*, Princeton, N.J.: Princeton University Press, 2009, pp. 87–107.

Freeman, Jody, and Andrew Guzman, "Climate Change and U.S. Interests," *Columbia Law Review*, Vol. 109, No. 6, October 2009, pp. 1531–1601. As of January 12, 2017:
http://www.jstor.org/stable/40380368

Frieden, J. A., and D. A. Lake, *International Political Economy: Perspectives on Global Power and Wealth*, 4th ed., London: Routledge, 2002.

Fuhrmann, Matthew, "Spreading Temptation: Proliferation and Peaceful Nuclear Cooperation Agreements," *International Security*, Vol. 34, No. 1, 2009, pp. 7–41.

Fuhrmann, Matthew, and Jeffrey D. Berejikian, "Disaggregating Noncompliance: Abstention versus Predation in the Nuclear Nonproliferation Treaty," *Journal of Conflict Resolution*, Vol. 56, No. 3, 2012, pp. 355–381.

Fuhrmann, Matthew, and Sarah Kreps, "Targeting Nuclear Programs in War and Peace: A Quantitative Empirical Analysis, 1941–2000," *Journal of Conflict Resolution*, Vol. 54, No. 6, 2010, pp. 831–859.

Fuhrmann, Matthew, and Lupu Yonatan, "Do Arms Control Treaties Work? Assessing the Effectiveness of the Nuclear Nonproliferation Treaty," *International Studies Quarterly*, Vol. 60, No. 3, September 2016, pp. 530–539.

Ganelli, Giovanni, and Juha Tervala, "Value of WTO Trade Agreements in a New Keynesian Model," IMF Working Paper WP/15/37, February 2015.

Gawande, Kishore, Bernard Hoekman, and Yue Cui, "Global Supply Chains and Trade Policy Responses to the 2009 Crisis," *World Bank Economic Review*, Vol. 29, No. 1, January 2015, pp. 102–128.

Germain, Randall, "Financial Order and World Politics: Crisis, Change and Continuity," *International Affairs*, Vol. 85, No. 4, 2009, pp. 669–687. As of January 26, 2017:
http://www.jstor.org/stable/27695085

Gilligan, Michael J., and Ernest J. Sergenti, "Do UN Interventions Cause Peace? Using Matching to Improve Causal Inference," *Quarterly Journal of Political Science*, Vol. 3, 2008, pp. 89–122.

Gilpin, Robert, *War and Change in World Politics*, New York: Cambridge University Press, 1983.

Glaser, Charles L., "Realists as Optimists: Cooperation as Self-Help," *International Security*, Vol. 19, No. 3, Winter 1994–1995, pp. 50–90.

———, *Rational Theory of International Politics: The Logic of Competition and Cooperation*, Princeton, N.J.: Princeton University Press, 2010.

Gleditsch, Kristian, and Michael Ward, "Diffusion and the International Context of Democratization," *International Organization*, Vol. 60, No. 4, Fall 2006, pp. 911–933.

Global Exchange, "How the International Monetary Fund and the World Bank Undermine Democracy and Erode Human Rights: Five Case Studies," *Global Exchange*, September 2001. As of January 26, 2017:
https://business-humanrights.org/en/how-the-international-monetary-fund-and-the-world-bank-undermine-democracy-and-erode-human-rights-five-case-studies-mexico-africa-brazil-colombia-haiti

Goldgeier, James M., and Michael McFaul, *Power and Purpose: U.S. Policy Toward Russia After the Cold War*, Washington, D.C.: Brookings Institution Press, 2003.

Goldstein, Judith L., Douglas Rivers, and Michael Tomz, "Institutions in International Relations: Understanding the Effects of the GATT and the WTO on World Trade," *International Organization*, Vol. 61, No. 1, 2007, pp. 37–67.

Goodliffe, Jay, and Darren Hawkins, "Explaining Commitment: States and the Convention Against Torture," *Journal of Politics*, Vol. 68, 2006, pp. 358–371.

Goodman, Ryan, and Derek Jinks, "How to Influence States: Socialization and International Human Rights Law," *Duke Law Journal*, Vol. 54, No. 3, December 2004, pp. 621–703.

Gowa, Joanne, and R. Hicks, "Politics, Institutions, and Trade: Lessons of the Interwar Era," *International Organization*, Vol. 67, No. 3, 2013, pp. 439–467.

Gowa, Joanne, and S. Y. Kim, "An Exclusive Country Club: The Effects of the GATT on Trade, 1950–94," *World Politics*, Vol. 57, No. 4, 2005, pp. 453–478.

Gowa, Joanne, and Edward D. Mansfield, "Power Politics and International Trade," *American Political Science Review*, Vol. 87, No. 2, 1993, pp. 408–420.

Gowan, Richard, "Peacekeeping at the Precipice: Is Everything Going Wrong for the UN?," background paper for the International Forum for the Challenges of Peace Operations, Beijing, October 2014. As of December 1, 2017:
http://cic.nyu.edu/sites/default/files/gowan_peacekeeping_at_the_precipice_-_background_paper_bejing_30sept2014.pdf

Granovetter, Mark, "Economic Action and Social Structure: The Problem of Embeddedness," *American Journal of Sociology*, Vol. 91, No. 3, 1985, pp. 481–510.

Gray, Julia, *The Company States Keep: International Economic Organizations and Investor Perceptions*, New York: Cambridge University Press, 2013.

Greenberg, Ezra, Martin Hirt, and Sven Smit, "The Global Forces Inspiring a New Narrative of Progress," *McKinsey Quarterly*, April 2017.

Greenberg, Jon, "How Much Does the United States Contribute to the UN?," *Politifact*, February 1, 2017.

Greenhill, Brian, "Recognition and Collective Identity Formation in International Politics," *European Journal of International Relations*, Vol. 14, No. 2, 2008, pp. 343–368.

Guzman, Andrew T., "A Compliance-Based Theory of International Law," *California Law Review*, Vol. 90, No. 6, December 2002, pp. 1823–1888.

Haass, Richard, *War of Necessity, War of Choice: A Memoir of Two Iraq Wars*, New York: Simon and Schuster, 2009.

Hafner-Burton, Emilie M., "Sticks and Stones: Naming and Shaming and the Human Rights Enforcement Problem," *International Organization*, Vol. 62, 2008, pp. 689–716.

———, *Forced to Be Good: Why Trade Agreements Boost Human Rights*, Ithaca, N.Y.: Cornell University Press, 2009.

———, "International Human Rights Regimes," *Annual Review of Political Science*, Vol. 15, 2012, pp. 265–286.

———, *Making Human Rights a Reality*, Princeton, N.J.: Princeton University Press, 2013.

Hafner-Burton, Emilie M., Miles Kahler, and Alexander H. Montgomery, "Network Analysis for International Relations," *International Organization*, Vol. 63, No. 3, Summer 2009, pp. 559–592.

Hafner-Burton, Emilie, Edward Mansfield, and Jon C. W. Pevehouse, "Human Rights Institutions, Sovereignty Costs, and Human Rights Outcomes," *British Journal of Political Science*, Vol. 45, No. 1, January 2015, pp. 1–27.

Hafner-Burton, Emilie M., and Kiyoteru Tsutsui, "Human Rights in a Globalizing World: The Paradox of Empty Promises," *American Journal of Sociology*, Vol. 110, 2005, pp. 1373–1411.

———, "Justice Lost! The Failure of International Human Rights Law to Matter Where Needed Most," *Journal of Peace Research*, Vol. 44, No. 4, 2007, pp. 407–425.

Hafner-Burton, Emilie M., Jana von Stein, and Erik Gartzke, "International Organizations Count," *Journal of Conflict Resolution*, Vol. 52, No. 2, April 2008, pp. 175–188.

Haggard, Stephen, and Beth A. Simmons, "Theories of International Regimes," *International Organization*, Vol. 41, No. 3, Summer 1987, pp. 491–517.

Hasenclever, Andreas, and Brigitte Weiffen, "International Institutions Are the Key: A New Perspective on the Democratic Peace," *Review of International Studies*, Vol. 32, No. 4, October 2006, pp. 563–585.

Hathaway, Oona, "Do Human Rights Treaties Make a Difference?," *Yale Law Journal*, Vol. 111, 2002, pp. 1935–2042.

———, "Why Do Countries Commit to Human Rights Treaties?," *Journal of Conflict Resolution*, Vol. 51, No. 4, 2007, pp. 588–621.

Hawkins, Darren, "Explaining Costly International Institutions: Persuasion and Enforceable Human Rights Norms," *International Studies Quarterly*, Vol. 48, No. 4, December 2004, pp. 779–804.

Heineman, Ben W., and Fritz Heimann, "The Long War Against Corruption," *Foreign Affairs*, Vol. 85, No. 3, 2006, pp. 75–86.

Helfer, Laurence R., and Erik Voeten, "International Courts as Agents of Legal Change: Evidence from LGBT Rights in Europe," *International Organization*, Vol. 68, Winter 2014, pp. 77–110.

Helleiner, Eric, "A Bretton Woods Moment? The 2007–2008 Crisis and the Future of Global Finance," *International Affairs*, Vol. 86, No. 3, 2010, pp. 619–636. As of January 26, 2017:
http://www.jstor.org/stable/40664271

Helm, Carstein, and Detlef Sprinz, "Measuring the Effectiveness of International Environmental Regimes," *Journal of Conflict Resolution*, Vol. 44, No. 5, October 2000, pp. 630–652.

Henderson, Conway W., "Conditions Affecting the Use of Political Repression," *Journal of Conflict Resolution*, Vol. 35, No. 1, 1991, pp. 120–142.

Hicks, Kathleen H., Michael J. Green, and Heather Conley, "Donald Trump Doesn't Understand the Value of U.S. Bases Overseas," *Foreign Policy*, April 7, 2016.

Hill, Daniel W., "Estimating the Effects of Human Rights Treaties on State Behavior," *Journal of Politics*, Vol. 72, No. 4, 2010, pp. 1161–1174.

Hisschemoller, Matthijs, and Joyeeta Gupta, "Problem-Solving Through International Environmental Agreements: The Issue of Regime Effectiveness," *International Political Science Review*, Vol. 20, No. 2, 1999, pp. 151–174.

Hollyer, James R., and Peter Rosendorff, "Why Do Authoritarian Regimes Sign the Convention Against Torture? Signaling, Domestic Politics and Non-Compliance," *Quarterly Journal of Political Science*, Vol. 6, Nos. 3–4, 2011, pp. 275–327.

Hoshi, Takeo, "Financial Regulation: Lessons from the Recent Financial Crises," *Journal of Economic Literature*, Vol. 49, No. 1, 2011, pp. 120–128. As of January 26, 2017:
http://www.jstor.org/stable/29779754

Hsu, Berry F. C., and Douglas W. Arner, "WTO Accession, Financial Reform and the Rule of Law in China," *China Review*, Vol. 7, No. 1, 2007, pp. 53–79.

Hu, Martin G., "WTO's Impact on the Rule of Law in China," in *The Rule of Law: Perspectives from the Pacific Rim*, Washington, D.C.: Mansfield Center for Pacific Affairs, 2000, pp. 101–106. As of November 9, 2017: http://www.mansfieldfdn.org/backup/programs/program_pdfs/08hu.pdf

Hug, Simon, and Simone Wegmann, "Complying with Human Rights," *International Interactions*, Vol. 42, No. 4, 2016, pp. 590–615. As of November 9, 2017: http://dx.doi.org/10.1080/03050629.2016.1185712

Hultman, Lisa, Jacob Kathman, and Megan Shannon, "United Nations Peacekeeping and Civilian Protection in Civil War," *American Journal of Political Science*, Vol. 57, No. 4, 2013, pp. 875–891.

Hymans, Jacques, *The Psychology of Nuclear Proliferation: Emotions, Identity, and Foreign Policy*, New York: Cambridge University Press, 2006.

Ikenberry, G. John, "Liberal Hegemony and the Future of American Postwar Order," in T. V. Paul and John Hall, eds., *International Order and the Future of World Politics*, Cambridge: Cambridge University Press, 1999, pp. 123–145.

———, *After Victory: Institutions, Strategic Restraint, and the Rebuilding of Order After Major Wars*, Princeton, N.J.: Princeton University Press, 2001.

———, *Liberal Leviathan: The Origins, Crisis, and Transformation of the American World Order*, Princeton, N.J.: Princeton University Press, 2011.

———, "The Future of the Liberal World Order," *Foreign Affairs*, May/June 2011. As of September 29, 2015: https://www.foreignaffairs.com/articles/2011-05-01/future-liberal-world-order

Ikenberry, G. John, and Charles A. Kupchan, "Socialization and Hegemonic Power," *International Organization*, Vol. 44, No. 3, Summer 1990, pp. 283–315.

International Monetary Fund, "Brazil: Helping Calm Financial Markets," November 21, 2007. As of November 9, 2017: https://www.imf.org/external/np/exr/articles/2007/112107.htm

———, "IMF's Response to the Global Economic Crisis," March 22, 2016. As of November 9, 2017: http://www.imf.org/en/About/Factsheets/Sheets/2016/07/27/15/19/Response-to-the-Global-Economic-Crisis

———, "Corruption: Costs and Mitigating Strategies," IMF Staff Discussion Note, May 2016.

———, "The Annual and Spring Meetings," fact sheet, April 19, 2017. As of November 9, 2017: http://www.imf.org/en/About/Factsheets/Annual-Spring-Meetings

Iriye, Akira, Petra Goedde, and William I. Hitchcock, eds., *The Human Rights Revolution: An International History*, New York: Oxford University Press, 2012.

Irwin, Douglas A., "The GATT's Contribution to Economic Recovery in Post-War Western Europe," National Bureau of Economic Research, Working Paper No. 44, December 1994.

———, The Welfare Cost of Autarky: Evidence from the Jeffersonian Trade Embargo, 1807–1809," *Review of International Economics*, Vol. 13, No. 4, 2005, pp. 631–645.

Isla, Nicholas, "Challenges to the BTWC, and Some Reasons for Optimism," International Network of Scientists and Engineers Against Proliferation, n.d. As of November 9, 2017:
http://www.inesap.org/bulletin-28/challenges-btwc-and-some-reasons-optimism

Jervis, Robert, "From Balance to Concert: A Study of International Security Cooperation," in Kenneth Oye, ed., *Cooperation Under Anarchy*, Princeton, N.J.: Princeton University Press, 1986, pp. 58–79.

———, *System Effects: Complexity in Political and Social Life*, Princeton, N.J.: Princeton University Press, 1997.

Jo, Dong Joon, and Erik Gartzke, "Determinants of Nuclear Weapons Proliferation," *Journal of Conflict Resolution*, Vol. 51, No. 1, 2007, pp. 167–194.

Johns, Leslie, and Lauren Peritz, "The Design of Trade Agreements," in Lisa L. Martin, ed., *The Oxford Handbook of the Political Economy of International Trade*, New York: Oxford University Press, 2015, pp. 337–359.

Johnson, A. Ross, and Misha Glenny, "Peacekeeping in the Balkans: An Assessment of the Decade," Wilson Center Explore Series No. 272, July 7, 2011.

Johnson, Jesse, and Brett Ashley Leeds, "Defense Pacts: A Prescription for Peace?," *Foreign Policy Analysis*, Vol. 7, No. 1, January 2011, pp. 45–65.

Johnston, Alastair Iain, "Treating International Institutions as Social Environments," *International Studies Quarterly*, Vol. 45, No. 4, December 2001, pp. 487–515.

———, *Social States: China and International Institutions, 1980–2000*, Princeton, N.J.: Princeton University Press, 2007.

Jolly, Richard, Louis Emmerji, and Thomas G. Weiss, *UN Ideas That Changed the World*. Bloomington: Indiana University Press, 2009.

Joyce, Joseph P., "Working Paper: Through a Glass Darkly: New Questions (and Answers) About IMF Programs," Wellesley College, June 2002. As of January 26, 2017:
https://pdfs.semanticscholar.org/45d4/f12955521c8fc107c7531a7218ed8f4331a2.pdf

Keck, Margaret E., and Kathryn Sikkink, "Transnational Advocacy Networks in International and Regional Politics," *International Social Science Journal*, Vol. 51, No. 159, 1999, pp. 89–101.

Kelemen, Daniel R., and David Vogel, "Trading Places: The Role of the United States and the European Union in International Environmental Politics," *Comparative Political Studies*, Vol. 43, No. 4, 2010, pp. 427–456. As of January 12, 2017: http://journals.sagepub.com/doi/pdf/10.1177/0010414009355265

Kelley, Judith, "Who Keeps International Commitments and Why? The International Criminal Court and Bilateral Nonsurrender Agreements," *American Political Science Review*, Vol. 101, No. 3, 2007, pp. 573–589.

Keohane, Robert O., *After Hegemony: Cooperation and Discord in the World Political Economy*, Princeton, N.J.: Princeton University Press, 1984.

———, *Power and Governance in a Partially Globalized World*, London: Routledge, 2002.

Keohane, Robert O., and Lisa L. Martin, "The Promise of Institutionalist Theory," *International Security*, Vol. 20, No. 1, Summer 1995, pp. 39–51.

Khaghaghordyan, Aram, "International Anti-Corruption Normative Framework: The State of the Art," Hertie School of Governance and European Commission, February 2014. As of November 9, 2017: http://anticorrp.eu/wp-content/uploads/2014/12/D1.1_Part3_International-Anti-corruption-Normative-Framework.pdf

Kilby, Christopher, "An Empirical Assessment of Informal Influence in the World Bank," *Economic Development and Cultural Change*, Vol. 61, No. 2, 2013, pp. 431–464. As of January 26, 2017: http://www.jstor.org/stable/10.1086/668278

Kim, Hunjoon, and Kathryn Sikkink, "Explaining the Deterrence Effect of Human Rights Prosecutions for Transitional Countries," *International Studies Quarterly*, Vol. 54, No. 4, 2010, pp. 939–963.

Kim, Soo Yeon, "Deep Integration and Regional Trade Agreements," in Lisa L. Martin, ed., *The Oxford Handbook of the Political Economy of International Trade*, New York: Oxford University Press, 2015, pp. 360–379.

Kinne, Brandon J. "Network Dynamics and the Evolution of International Cooperation," *American Political Science Review*, Vol. 107, No. 4, November 2013, pp. 766–785.

Kirschner, Jonathan, "International Relations Then and Now: Why the Great Recession Was Not the Great Depression," *History of Economic Ideas*, Vol. 22, No. 3, 2014.

Kissinger, Henry, *World Order*, New York: Penguin, 2014.

Knowledge@Wharton, "NAFTA's Impact on the U.S. Economy: What Are the Facts?" September 6, 2016. As of November 14, 2017: http://knowledge.wharton.upenn.edu/article/nafras-impact-u-s-economy-facts/

Koh, Harold, "Why Do Nations Obey International Law?," *Yale Law Journal*, Vol. 106, 1996–1997, pp. 2599–2659.

Koremenos, Barbara, Charles Lipson, and Duncan Snidal, "The Rational Design of International Institutions," *International Organization*, Vol. 55, No. 4, Autumn 2001, pp. 761–799.

Krasner, Stephen D., "Structural Causes and Regime Consequences: Regimes as Intervening Variables," *International Organization*, Vol. 36, No. 2, Spring 1982, pp. 185–205.

———, "Global Communications and National Power: Life on the Pareto Frontier," *World Politics*, Vol. 43, No. 3, 1993, pp. 336–366.

Krepon, Michael, and Samuel Black, "Good News and Bad News on the NPT," *Arms Control Today*, March 4, 2010. As of December 3, 2016: https://www.armscontrol.org/act/2010_03/LookingBack

Kroenig, Matthew, "Importing the Bomb: Sensitive Nuclear Assistance and Nuclear Proliferation," *Journal of Conflict Resolution*, Vol. 53, No. 2, 2009, pp. 161–180.

Krol, Robert, "Trade, Protectionism, and the U.S. Economy: Examining the Evidence," Washington, D.C.: The CATO Institute, September 16, 2008.

Krueger, Anne O., "An Enduring Need: The Importance of Multilateralism in the 21st Century," remarks, International Monetary Fund, September 19, 2006.

Kupchan, Charles A., "Unpacking Hegemony: The Social Foundations of Hierarchical Order," in G. John Ikenberry, ed., *Power, Order, and Change in World Politics*, Cambridge: Cambridge University Press, 2014, pp. 19–60.

Lake, David A., "Dominance and Subordination in World Politics," in G. John Ikenberry, ed., *Power, Order, and Change in World Politics*, Cambridge: Cambridge University Press, 2014, pp. 61–82.

Landman, Todd, *Protecting Human Rights: A Comparative Study*, Washington, D.C.: Georgetown University Press, 2005.

Larson, Deborah Welch, and Alexei Shevchenko, "Status Seekers: Chinese and Russian Responses to U.S. Primacy," *International Security*, Vol. 34, No. 4, Spring 2010, pp. 63–95.

Lebovic, James H., and Erik Voeten, "The Cost of Shame: International Organizations and Foreign Aid in the Punishing of Human Rights Violators," *Journal of Peace Research*, Vol. 46, No. 1, 2009, pp. 79–97.

Lebow, Richard Ned, "*Thumos*, War, and Peace," *Common Knowledge*, Vol. 21, No. 1, 2014, pp. 50–82.

Leeds, Brett Ashley, "Domestic Political Institutions, Credible Commitments, and International Cooperation," *American Journal of Political Science*, Vol. 43, No. 4, 1999, pp. 979–1002.

———, "Do Alliances Deter Aggression? The Influence of Military Alliances on the Initiation of Militarized Interstate Disputes," *American Journal of Political Science*, Vol. 47, No. 3, July 2003a, pp. 427–439.

———, "Alliance Reliability in Times of War: Explaining State Decisions to Violate Treaties," *International Organization*, Vol. 57, No. 4, Autumn 2003b, pp. 801–827.

Leipziger, Danny, "The Role and Influence of International Financial Institutions," in Bruce Currie-Alder, Ravi Kanbur, David M. Malone, and Rohinton Medhora, eds., *International Development: Ideas, Experience, and Prospects*, Oxford: Oxford University Press, 2014.

Lektzian, David J., and Christopher M. Sprecher, "Sanctions, Signals, and Militarized Conflict," *American Journal of Political Science*, Vol. 51, No. 2, 2007, pp. 415–431.

Li, Liao, and Yu Minyou, "Impact of the WTO on China's Rule of Law in Trade," *Journal of World Trade*, Vol. 49, No. 5, 2015, pp. 837–872.

Lim, Daniel Yew Mao, and James Raymond Vreeland, "Regional Organizations and International Politics: Japanese Influence over the Asian Development Bank and the UN Security Council," *World Politics*, Vol. 65, No. 1, 2013, pp. 34–72.

Limão, N., "Preferential Trade Agreements as Stumbling Blocks for Multilateral Trade Liberalization: Evidence for the United States," *American Economic Review*, Vol. 96, No. 3, 2006, pp. 896–914.

Lindner, Samira, *Literature Review on Social Norms and Corruption*, London: Transparency International, January 2014.

Linos, Katerina, "Diffusion Through Democracy," *American Journal of Political Science*, Vol. 55, No. 3, 2011, pp. 678–695.

Lipscy, Phillip Y., "Japan's Asian Monetary Fund Proposal," *Stanford Journal of East Asian Affairs*, Vol. 3, No. 1, 2003, pp. 93–104.

———, "Explaining Institutional Change: Policy Areas, Outside Options, and the Bretton Woods Institutions," *American Journal of Political Science*, Vol. 59, No. 2, April 2015, pp. 341–356.

Lipson, Michael, "Transaction Cost Estimation and International Regimes: Of Crystal Balls and Sheriff's Posses," *International Studies Review*, Vol. 6, No. 1, 2004, pp. 1–20.

Lostumbo, Michael J., Michael J. McNerney, Eric Peltz, Derek Eaton, David R. Frelinger, Victoria A. Greenfield, John Halliday, Patrick Mills, Bruce R. Nardulli, Stacie L. Pettyjohn, Jerry M. Sollinger, and Stephen M. Worman, *Overseas Basing of U.S. Military Forces: An Assessment of Relative Costs and Strategic Benefits*, Santa Monica, Calif.: RAND Corporation, RR-201-OSD, 2013.

Lupu, Yonatan, "The Informative Power of Treaty Commitment: Using the Spatial Model to Address Selection Effects," *American Journal of Political Science*, Vol. 57, No. 4, 2013, pp. 912–925.

Mallaby, Sebastian, *The World's Banker: A Story of Failed States, Financial Crises, and the Wealth and Poverty of Nations*, New York: Penguin Press, 2004.

Maggi, Giovanni, "The Role of Multilateral Institutions in International Trade Cooperation," *American Economic Review*, Vol. 89, No. 1, March 1999, pp. 190–214.

Maggi, Giovanni, and Andres Rodriguez-Clare, "The Value of Trade Agreements in the Presence of Political Pressures," *Journal of Political Economy*, Vol. 106, No. 3, 1998, pp. 574–601.

Mansfield, E. D., and E. Reinhardt, "Multilateral Determinants of Regionalism: The Effects of GATT/WTO on the Formation of Preferential Trading Arrangements," *International Organization*, Vol. 57, No. 4, 2003, pp. 829–862.

———, "International Institutions and the Volatility of International Trade," *International Organization*, Vol. 62, No. 4, 2008, 621–652.

Martin, Lisa L., "Against Compliance," unpublished manuscript, December 2009. As of November 9, 2017: https://papers.ssrn.com/sol3/papers.cfm?abstract_id=1900163

———, "Against Compliance," in Jeffrey L. Dunoff and Mark A. Pollack, eds., *Interdisciplinary Perspectives on International Law and International Relations: The State of the Art*, New York: Cambridge University Press, 2013, pp. 591–610.

———, ed., *The Oxford Handbook of the Political Economy of International Trade*, New York: Oxford University Press, 2015.

Martin, Lisa L., and Beth A. Simmons, "Theories and Empirical Studies of International Institutions," *International Organization*, Vol. 52, No. 4, 1998, pp. 729–757.

Mazarr, Michael J., "Preserving the Post-War Order," *Washington Quarterly*, Vol. 40, No. 2, Summer 2017, pp. 29–49.

Mazarr, Michael J., Astrid Cevallos, Miranda Priebe, Andrew Radin, Kathleen Reedy, Alexander D. Rothenberg, Julia A. Thompson, and Jordan Willcox, *Measuring the Health of the Liberal International Order*, Santa Monica, Calif.: RAND Corporation, 2017.

Mazarr, Michael J., Miranda Priebe, Andrew Radin, and Astrid Stuth Cevallos, *Understanding the Current International Order*, Santa Monica, Calif.: RAND Corporation, 2016.

McCoy, Jennifer L., and Heather Heckel, "The Emergence of a Global Anti-Corruption Norm," *International Politics*, Vol. 38, No. 1, 2001, pp. 65–90.

Mearsheimer, John J., "The Case for a Ukrainian Nuclear Deterrent," *Foreign Affairs*, Vol. 72, No. 3, 1993, pp. 50–66.

———, "The False Promise of International Institutions," *International Security*, Vol. 19, No. 3, 1994, pp. 5–49.

Medeiros, Evan S., Keith Crane, Eric Heginbotham, Norman D. Levin, Julia F. Lowell, Angel Rabasa, and Somi Seong, *Pacific Currents: The Responses of U.S. Allies and Security Partners in East Asia to China's Rise*, Santa Monica, Calif.: RAND Corporation, MG-736-AF, 2008.

Meyer, Stephen, *The Dynamics of Nuclear Proliferation*, Chicago: University of Chicago Press, 1984.

Miller, Nicholas L., "The Secret Success of Nonproliferation Sanctions," *International Organization*, Vol. 68, No. 4, 2014, pp. 913–944.

Miller, Steven E., "Skepticism Triumphant: The Bush Administration and the Waning of Arms Control," *La Revue Internationale et Strategique*, Vol. 51, 2003, pp. 13–36.

Milner, Helen V., "Globalization, Development, and International Institutions: Normative and Positive Perspectives," *Perspectives on Politics*, Vol. 3, No. 4, December 2005, pp. 833–854.

Mishkin, Frederic S., "Why We Shouldn't Turn Our Backs on Financial Globalization," *IMF Staff Papers*, Vol. 56, No. 1, 2009, pp. 139–170. As of January 26, 2017:
http://www.jstor.org/stable/40377801

Mistry, Percy S., "International Financial Institutions and Their Leaders," *Economic and Political Weekly*, Vol. 42, No. 26, 2007, pp. 2508–2513. As of January 26, 2017:
http://www.jstor.org/stable/4419756

Mitchell, Ronald B., *Intentional Oil Pollution at Sea: Environmental Policy and Treaty Compliance*, Cambridge, Mass.: MIT Press, 1994.

———, "A Quantitative Approach to Evaluating International Environmental Regimes," in Arild Underdal and Oran Young, eds., *Regime Consequences: Methodological Challenges and Research Strategies*, Dordrecht: Kluwer Academic Publishers, 2004, pp. 121–149.

Mitchell, Sara McLaughlin, and Paul R. Hensel, "International Institutions and Compliance with Agreements," *American Journal of Political Science*, Vol. 51, No. 4, 2007, pp. 721–737.

Monath, Thomas P., and Lance K. Gordon, "Strengthening the Biological Weapons Convention," *Science*, Vol. 282, No. 5393, 1998, p. 1423.

Monteiro, Nuno P., and Alexandre Debs, "The Strategic Logic of Nuclear Proliferation," *International Security*, Vol. 39, No. 2, 2014, pp. 7–51.

Moravcsik, Andrew, "Taking Preferences Seriously: A Liberal Theory of International Politics," *International Organization*, Vol. 51, No. 4, Autumn 1997, pp. 513–553.

Moroney, Jennifer D. P., Kim Cragin, Eric Stephen Gons, Beth Grill, John E. Peters, and Rachel M. Swanger, *International Cooperation with Partner Air Forces*, Santa Monica, Calif.: RAND Corporation, MG-790-AF, 2009.

Moroney, Jennifer D. P., Adam R. Grissom, and Jefferson P. Marquis, *A Capabilities-Based Strategy for Army Security Cooperation*, Santa Monica, Calif.: RAND Corporation, MG-563-A, 2007.

Murdie, Amanda M., and David R. Davis, "Shaming and Blaming: Using Events Data to Assess the Impact of Human Rights INGOs," *International Studies Quarterly*, Vol. 56, No. 1, 2012, pp. 1–16.

Murdoch, James C., Todd Sandler, and Wim P. M. Vijverberg, "The Participation Decision Versus the Level of Participation in an Environmental Treaty: A Spatial Probit Analysis," *Journal of Public Economics*, Vol. 87, 2003, pp. 337–362.

Nadelmann, Ethan A., "Global Prohibition Regimes: The Evolution of Norms in International Society," *International Organization*, Vol. 44, No. 4, Autumn 1990, pp. 479–526.

Nelson, Rebecca M., "Multilateral Development Banks: U.S. Contributions, FY2000–FY2016," Congressional Research Service, March 20, 2017.

Neumayer, Eric, "Do International Human Rights Treaties Improve Respect for Human Rights?," *Journal of Conflict Resolution*, Vol. 49, 2005, pp. 925–953.

Noland, Marcus, Gary Clyde Hufbauer, Sherman Robinson, and Tyler Moran, *Assessing Trade Agendas in the U.S. Presidential Campaign*, Briefing 16-6, Washington, D.C.: Peterson Institute for International Economics, September 2016.

Nye, Joseph S., "Maintaining a Nonproliferation Regime," *International Organization*, Vol. 35, No. 1, 1981, pp. 15–38.

Ossa, Ralph, "Trade Wars and Trade Talks with Data," National Bureau of Economic Research, Working Paper No. 17347, 2011. As of November 20, 2017: https://core.ac.uk/download/pdf/6538043.pdf

Oye, Kenneth, ed., *Cooperation Under Anarchy*, Princeton, N.J.: Princeton University Press, 1986.

Pape, Robert A., "Soft Balancing Against the United States," *International Security*, Vol. 30, No. 1, Summer 2005, pp. 7–45.

Paris, Roland, "Saving Liberal Peacebuilding," *Review of International Studies*, Vol. 36, No. 2, 2010, pp. 337–365.

———, "Peacekeeping Works Better Than You May Think," *Political Violence @ a Glance* blog, August 12, 2014. As of November 14, 2017: http://politicalviolenceataglance.org/2014/08/12/peacekeeping-works-better-than-you-may-think/

Park, Han S., "Correlates of Human Rights: Global Tendencies," *Human Rights Quarterly*, Vol. 9, No. 3, 1987, pp. 405–413.

Patrick, Stewart, *The Best Laid Plans: The Origins of American Multilateralism and the Dawn of the Cold War*, Lanham, Md.: Rowman and Littlefield, 2009.

Paul, T. V., *The Tradition of Non-Use of Nuclear Weapons*, Stanford, Calif.: Stanford University Press, 2009.

Pevehouse, Jon C., "Democracy from the Outside-In? International Organizations and Democratization," *International Organization*, Vol. 56, No. 3, 2002, pp. 515–549.

Pevehouse, Jon C., and Bruce Russett, "Democratic International Governmental Organizations Promote Peace," *International Organization*, Vol. 60, No. 4, 2006, pp. 969–1000.

Pierson, Paul, "Increasing Returns, Path Dependence, and the Study of Politics," *American Political Science Review*, Vol. 94, No. 2, June 2000, pp. 251–267.

Poe, Steven C., Sabine C. Carey, and Tanya C. Vázquez, "How Are These Pictures Different? A Quantitative Comparison of the US State Department and Amnesty International Human Rights Reports, 1976–1995," *Human Rights Quarterly*, Vol. 23, No. 3, 2001, pp. 650–677.

Poe, Steven C., and C. Neal Tate, "Repression of Human Rights to Personal Integrity in the 1980s: A Global Analysis," *American Political Science Review*, Vol. 88, 1994, pp. 853–872.

Poe, Steven C., C. Neal Tate, and Linda Camp Keith, "Repression of the Human Right to Personal Integrity Revisited: A Global Cross-National Study Covering the Years 1976–1993," *International Studies Quarterly*, Vol. 43, No. 2, 1999, pp. 291–313.

Porter, Tony, "Why International Institutions Matter in the Global Credit Crisis," *Global Governance*, Vol. 15, No. 1, January–March 2009, pp. 3–8.

Posen, Barry R., *Restraint: A New Foundation for U.S. Grand Strategy*, Ithaca, N.Y.: Cornell University Press, 2014.

Potter, William C., "The NPT and the Sources of Nuclear Restraint," *Daedalus*, Vol. 139, No. 1, Winter 2010, pp. 68–81.

———. "The High Costs and Limited Benefits of America's Military Alliances," *The National Interest*, August 7, 2016.

Preble, Christopher, "The Costs of Our Overseas Military Presence," Cato Institute, April 17, 2013.

Price, Richard M., *The Chemical Weapons Taboo*, Ithaca, N.Y.: Cornell University Press, 2007.

Rathbun, Brian C., "Uncertain About Uncertainty: Understanding the Multiple Meanings of a Crucial Concept in International Relations Theory," *International Studies Quarterly*, Vol. 51, No. 3, September 2007, pp. 533–557.

———, "Before Hegemony: Generalized Trust and the Creation and Design of International Security Organizations," *International Organization*, Vol. 65, No. 2, Spring 2011, pp. 243–273.

Raustiala, Kal, "The Architecture of International Cooperation," *Virginia Journal of International Law*, Vol. 43, 2002–2003, pp. 1–93.

Raustiala, Kal, and David G. Victor, "The Regime Complex for Plant Genetic Resources," *International Organization*, Vol. 58, No. 2, pp. 277–309.

Reiter, Dan, "Security Commitments and Nuclear Proliferation," *Foreign Policy Analysis*, Vol. 10, No. 1, 2014, pp. 61–80.

Richards, David L., Alyssa Webb, and K. Chad Clay, "Respect for Physical Integrity Rights in the 21st Century: Evaluating Poe & Tate's Model 20 Years Later," *Journal of Human Rights*, Vol. 14, 2015, pp. 291–311.

Ringquist, Evan J., and Tatiana Kostadinova, "Assessing the Effectiveness of International Environmental Agreements: The Case of the 1985 Helsinki Protocol," *American Journal of Political Science*, Vol. 49, No. 1, 2005, pp. 86–102. As of January 12, 2017:
http://www.jstor.org/stable/3647715

Ristau, Bruno A., Ugljesa Zvekic, and Mary Ellen Warlow, "International Cooperation and Transnational Organized Crime," *Proceedings of the Annual Meeting (American Society of International Law)*, Vol. 90, 1996, pp. 533–541.

Roach, J. Ashley, "Countering Piracy off Somalia: International Law and International Institutions," *American Journal of International Law*, Vol. 104, No. 3, July 2010, pp. 397–416.

Roberts, J. Timmons, Bradley C. Parks, and Alexis A. Vasquez, "Who Ratified Environmental Treaties and Why? Institutionalism, Structuralism, and Participation by 192 Nations in 22 Treaties," *Global Environmental Politics*, Vol. 4, No. 3, August 2004, pp. 22–64. As of January 12, 2017:
https://www.wm.edu/offices/itpir/_documents/aiddata/who_ratifies_2004.pdf

Robinson, J. P. Perry, "Implementing the Chemical Weapons Convention," *International Affairs*, Vol. 72, No. 1, 1996, pp. 73–89.

Rogoff, Kenneth, "Who Needs the IMF," Brookings Institution, September 25, 2006.

Romaniuk, Peter, "Institutions as Swords and Shields: Multilateral Counter-Terrorism Since 9/11," *Review of International Studies*, Vol. 36, No. 3, 2010, pp. 591–613.

Rose, Andrew K., "Do We Really Know That the WTO Increases Trade?," National Bureau of Economic Research, Working Paper 9273, October 2004.

———, "Does the WTO Make Trade More Stable?," *Open Economies Review*, Vol. 16, No. 1, 2005, pp. 7–22.

———, "The International Economic Order in the Aftermath of the 'Great Recession': A Cautious Case for Optimism," *Brown Journal of World Affairs*, Vol. 16, No. 2, Spring–Summer 2010, pp. 169–178.

Rose, Cecily, *International Anti-Corruption Norms: Their Creation and Influence on Domestic Legal Systems*, Oxford: Oxford University Press, 2015.

Rose, Gideon, "What Obama Gets Right: Keep Calm and Carry the Liberal Order On," *Foreign Affairs*, Vol. 94, No. 5, September–October 2015, pp. 2–12.

Roselli, A., *Money and Trade Wars in Interwar Europe*, Basingstoke, U.K.: Palgrave Macmillan, 2014.

Rublee, Maria Rost, "Taking Stock of the Nuclear Nonproliferation Regime: Using Social Psychology to Understand Regime Effectiveness," *International Studies Review*, Vol. 10, No. 3, 2008, pp. 420–450.

———, *Nonproliferation Norms: Why States Choose Nuclear Restraint*, Athens: University of Georgia Press, 2009.

Ruggie, John Gerard, "International Regimes, Transactions, and Change: Embedded Liberalism in the Postwar Economic Order," *International Organization*, Vol. 36, No. 2, Spring 1982, pp. 379–415.

———, ed., *Multilateralism Matters: The Theory and Praxis of an Institutional Form*, New York: Columbia University Press, 1993.

———, "Third Try at World Order? America and Multilateralism After the Cold War," *Political Science Quarterly*, Vol. 109, No. 4, Autumn 1994, pp. 553–570.

———, "The False Premise of Realism," *International Security*, Vol. 20, No. 1, Summer 1995, pp. 62–70.

———, *Winning the Peace: America and World Order in the New Era*, New York: Columbia University Press, 1996.

Russett, Bruce, John R. Oneal, and David R. Davis, "The Third Leg of the Kantian Tripod for Peace: International Organizations and Militarized Disputes, 1950–85," *International Organization*, Vol. 52, No. 3, 1998, pp. 441–467.

Sachs, Jeffrey D., *The End of Poverty: Economic Possibilities for Our Time*, New York: Penguin Press, 2005.

Sagan, Scott D., "Why Do States Build Nuclear Weapons? Three Models in Search of a Bomb," *International Security*, Vol. 21, No. 3, 1996, pp. 54–86.

———, "The Causes of Nuclear Weapons Proliferation," *Annual Review of Political Science*, Vol. 17, No. 14, 2011, pp. 225–241.

Sagan, Scott D., and Kenneth N. Waltz, *The Spread of Nuclear Weapons: A Debate Renewed*, 2nd ed., New York: Norton, 2003.

Samaan, Andrew Watson, "Enforcement of International Environmental Treaties: An Analysis," *Fordham Environmental Law Review*, Vol. 5, No. 1, 2011, pp. 261–283.

Samans, Richard, Klaus Schwab, and Mark Malloch-Brown, "Running the World, After the Crash," *Foreign Policy*, No. 184, 2011, pp. 80–83. As of January 26, 2017: http://www.jstor.org/stable/41233407

Sambanis, Nicholas, "Short-Term and Long-Term Effects of United Nations Peace Operations," *World Bank Economic Review*, Vol. 22, 2008, pp. 9–32.

Sandholtz, Wayne, and Mark M. Gray, "International Integration and National Corruption," *International Organization*, Vol. 57, No. 4, 2003, pp. 761–800.

Schmidt, Andreas, and Harald Muller, "The Little-Known Story of De-Proliferation: Why States Give Up Nuclear Weapons Activities," in William Potter and Gaukhar Mukhatzhanova, eds., *Forecasting Nuclear Proliferation in the 21st Century*, Stanford, Calif.: Stanford University Press, 2010, pp. 124–158.

Schroeder, Paul W., "The 19th Century International System: Changes in the Structure," *World Politics*, Vol. 39, No. 1, October 1986, pp. 1–26.

Schweller, Randall L., "The Problem of International Order Revisited," *International Security*, Vol. 26, No. 1, Summer 2001, pp. 161–186.

Seelarbokus, Chenaz B., "Assessing the Effectiveness of International Environmental Agreements (IEAs): Demystifying the Issue of Data Unavailability," *SAGE Open*, Vol. 4, No. 1, January–March 2014, pp. 1–18. As of January 12, 2017: http://journals.sagepub.com/doi/abs/10.1177/2158244014521820

Shamat, Patricia, "Name and Shame: Unravelling the Stigmatization of Weapons of Mass Destruction," *Contemporary Security Policy*, Vol. 36, No. 1, 2015, pp. 104–122.

Shanks, C., H. K. Jacobson, and J. H. Kaplan, "Inertia and Change in the Constellation of International Governmental Organizations, 1981–1992," *International Organization*, Vol. 50, No. 4, 1996, pp. 593–627.

Shannon, Megan, Daniel Morey, and Frederick J. Boehmke, "The Influence of International Organizations on Militarized Dispute Initiation and Duration," *International Studies Quarterly*, Vol. 54, No. 4, 2010, pp. 1123–1141.

Shelburne, Robert C., "The Global Financial Crisis and Its Impact on Trade: The World and European Emerging Economies," United Nations Economic Commission for Europe Discussion Paper Series, No. 2, September 2010.

Simmons, Beth, "The International Politics of Harmonization: The Case of Capital Market Regulation," *International Organization*, Vol. 55, No. 3, 2001, pp. 589–620.

———, "Capacity, Commitment, and Compliance: International Institutions and Territorial Disputes," *Journal of Conflict Resolution*, Vol. 46, No. 6, December 2002, pp. 829–856.

———, "Rules over Real Estate: Trade, Territorial Conflict, and International Borders as Institution," *Journal of Conflict Resolution*, Vol. 49, No. 6, December 2005, pp. 823–848.

———, *Mobilizing for Human Rights: International Law in Domestic Politics*, New York: Cambridge University Press, 2009.

———, "Treaty Compliance and Violation," *Annual Review of Political Science*, Vol. 13, No. 1, 2010, pp. 273–296.

Simmons, Beth A., and Allison Danner, "Credible Commitments and the International Criminal Court," *International Organization*, Vol. 64, No. 2, 2010, pp. 225–256.

Simmons, Beth A., Frankl Dobbin, and Geoffrey Garrett, "Introduction: The International Diffusion of Liberalism," *International Organization*, Vol. 60, Fall 2006, pp. 781–810.

Simmons, Beth A., and Daniel J. Hopkins, "The Constraining Power of International Treaties: Theory and Methods," *American Political Science Review*, Vol. 99, 2005, pp. 623–631.

Singh, Sonali, and Christopher R. Way, "The Correlates of Nuclear Proliferation: A Quantitative Test," *Journal of Conflict Resolution*, Vol. 48, No. 6, 2004, pp. 859–885.

Smith-Cannoy, Heather, *Insincere Commitments: Human Rights Treaties, Abusive States, and Citizen Activism*, Washington, D.C.: Georgetown University Press, 2012.

Snyder, Quddus Z., "Integrating Rising Powers: Liberal Systemic Theory and the Mechanism of Cooperation," *Review of International Studies*, Vol. 39, 2013a, pp. 209–231.

———, "Taking the System Seriously: Another Liberal Theory of International Politics," *International Studies Review*, Vol. 15, 2013b, pp. 539–561.

Solingen, Etel, *Nuclear Logics: Contrasting Paths in East Asia and the Middle East*, Princeton, N.J.: Princeton University Press, 2007.

Staiger, Robert W., "Report on the International Trade Regime for the International Task Force on Global Public Goods," unpublished paper, February 5, 2004. As of November 9, 2017:
http://www.dartmouth.edu/~rstaiger/global.public.goods.paper.020504.pdf

Staiger, Robert W., and Guido Tabellini, "Do GATT Rules Help Governments Make Domestic Commitments?," *Economics and Politics*, Vol. 11, No. 2, July 1999, pp. 109–144.

Standards Australia, "The Economic Benefits of Standardisation," n.d. As of November 9, 2017:
http://www.standards.org.au/OurOrganisation/News/Documents/
Economic%20Benefits%20of%20Standardisation.pdf

Stiglitz, Joseph E., *Globalization and Its Discontents*, New York: Norton, 2002.

Stone, Randall W., *Controlling Institutions: International Organizations and the Global Economy*, New York: Cambridge University Press, 2011.

Strauss-Kahn, Dominique, "Multilateralism and the Role of the International Monetary Fund in the Global Financial Crisis," International Monetary Fund, April 23, 2009. As of December 1, 2017:
https://www.imf.org/en/News/Articles/2015/09/28/04/53/sp042309

Subramanian, Arvind, and Shang-Jin Wei, "The WTO Promotes Trade, Strongly but Unevenly," *Journal of International Economics*, Vol. 72, No. 1, 2007, pp. 151–175.

Sussman, Glen, "The USA and Global Environmental Policy: Domestic Constraints on Effective Leadership," *International Political Science Review*, Vol. 25, No. 4, 2004, pp. 349–369. As of January 12, 2017:
http://journals.sagepub.com/doi/pdf/10.1177/0192512104045077

Tankersley, Jim, "Donald Trump's Trade War Could Kill Millions of U.S. Jobs," *The Washington Post*, March 25, 2016. As of November 20, 2017:
https://www.washingtonpost.com/news/wonk/wp/2016/03/25/donald-trumps-trade-war-could-kill-millions-of-u-s-jobs/?utm_term=.7c8d8fd7501b

Tannenwald, Nina, *The Nuclear Taboo: The United States and the Nonuse of Nuclear Weapons Since 1945*, New York: Cambridge University Press, 2007.

Tarini, Gabrielle, "Keeping the Biological Weapons Convention Relevant," *Bulletin of the Atomic Scientists*, November 1, 2016. As of December 1, 2017:
http://thebulletin.org/keeping-biological-weapons-convention-relevant10093

Thornberry, Cedric, "Look at the Benefits and Costs of Peacekeeping," *New York Times*, June 11, 1998.

Tomz, M., J. L. Goldstein, and D. Rivers, "Do We Really Know That the WTO Increases Trade? Comment," *American Economic Review*, Vol. 97, No. 5, December 2007, pp. 2005–2018.

Tucker, Jonathan B. "The Chemical Weapons Convention: Has It Enhanced U.S. Security?," *Arms Control Today*, April 2001. As of December 1, 2017:
https://www.armscontrol.org/act/2001_04/tucker

UNCTAD, "International Trade After the Economic Crisis: Challenges and New Opportunities," United Nations, 2010.

United Nations, "Financing Peacekeeping," n.d.a. As of November 9, 2017:
http://www.un.org/en/peacekeeping/operations/financing.shtml

———, "History of Peacekeeping," n.d.b. As of December 28, 2016:
http://www.un.org/en/peacekeeping/operations/history.shtml

———, "List of Peacekeeping Operations, 1948–2013," n.d.c. As of November 9, 2017
http://www.un.org/en/peacekeeping/documents/operationslist.pdf

———, "The Rule of Law in the UN's Intergovernmental Work," n.d.d. As of November 9, 2017:
https://www.un.org/ruleoflaw/what-is-the-rule-of-law/the-rule-of-law-in-un-work/

———, "Guidance Note of the Secretary-General: The UN Approach to Rule of Law Assistance," April 2008. As of November 9, 2017:
https://www.un.org/ruleoflaw/files/RoL%20Guidance%20Note%20UN%20Approach%20FINAL.pdf

———, "Human Rights Bodies," United Nations Office of the High Commissioner for Human Rights, 2011. As of November 9, 2017: http://www.ohchr.org/EN/HRBodies/Pages/HumanRightsBodies.aspx

U.S. Department of Defense, "Estimated Cost to Each U.S. Taxpayer of Each of the Wars in Afghanistan, Iraq and Syria," July 2017. As of November 20, 2017: http://www.govexec.com/media/gbc/docs/pdf_edit/section_1090_fy17_ndaa_cost_of_wars_to_per_taxpayer-july_2017.pdf

U.S. Department of State, *United States Contributions to International Organizations: Sixty-Fifth Annual Report to the Congress, Fiscal Year 2016*, Washington, D.C.: U.S. Department of State, n.d.

———, *Department of State, Foreign Operations and Related Programs: Congressional Budget Justification, Fiscal Year 2018*, Washington, D.C.: U.S. Department of State, May 23, 2017.

U.S. Department of the Treasury, *United States Participation in the Multilateral Development Banks in the 1980s*, Washington, D.C.: U.S. Department of the Treasury, February 1982.

U.S. General Accounting Office, "Allied Contributions in Support of Operations Desert Shield and Desert Storm," July 31, 1991.

"U.S. Rejection of Protocol to Biological Weapons Convention," *American Journal of International Law*, Vol. 95, No. 4, 2001, pp. 899–901.

Van Baaren, Rick B., Rob W. Holland, Kerry Kawakami, and Ad van Knippenberg, "Mimicry and Prosocial Behavior," *Psychological Science*, Vol. 15, No. 1, January 2004, pp. 71–74.

Van der Lijn, Jair, Ivan Briscoe, Margriet Drent, Kees Homan, Frans-Paul van der Puten, and Dick Zandee, *Peacekeeping Operations in a Changing World*, The Hague: Netherlands Institute of International Relations, January 2015.

Vannoorenberghe, G., "Firm-Level Volatility and Exports," *Journal of International Economics*, Vol. 86, No. 1, 2012, pp. 57–67.

Vaubel, Roland, "A Public Choice Approach to International Organization," *Public Choice*, Vol. 51, 1986, pp. 39–57.

Voeten, Erik, "Why No UN Security Council Reform? Lessons for and from Institutionalist Theory," in Dimitris Bourantonis, Kostas Ifantis, and Panayotis Tsakonas, eds., *Multilateralism and Security Institutions in an Era of Globalization*, New York: Routledge, 2008, pp. 288–305.

———, "The Impartiality of International Judges: Evidence from the European Court of Human Rights," *American Political Science Review*, Vol. 102, 2008, pp. 417–433.

Von Stein, Jana, "Do Treaties Constrain or Screen? Selection Bias and Treaty Compliance," *American Political Science Review*, Vol. 99, 2005, pp. 611–622.

———, "The International Law and Politics of Climate Change: Ratification of the United Nations Framework Convention and the Kyoto Protocol," *Journal of Conflict Resolution*, Vol. 52, No. 2, April 2008, pp. 243–268. As of January 12, 2017: http://journals.sagepub.com/doi/pdf/10.1177/0022002707313692

Vreeland, James Raymond, "Why Do Governments and the IMF Enter into Agreements? Statistically Selected Cases," *International Political Science Review/ Revue Internationale de Science Politique*, Vol. 24, No. 3, 2003, pp. 321–343.

———, "Political Institutions and Human Rights: Why Dictatorships Enter into the United Nations Convention Against Torture," *International Organization*, Vol. 62, 2008, pp. 65–101.

Vreeland, James Raymond, and Axel Dreher, *The Political Economy of the United Nations Security Council: Money and Influence*, New York: Cambridge University Press, 2014.

Walsh, James I., "National Preferences and International Institutions: Evidence from European Monetary Integration," *International Studies Quarterly*, Vol. 45, No. 1, March 2001, pp. 59–80.

Ward, Hugh, "International Linkages and Environmental Sustainability: The Effectiveness of the Regime Network," *Journal of Peace Research*, Vol. 43, No. 2, 2006, pp. 149–166. As of January 12, 2017: http://www.jstor.org/stable/27640283

Way, Christopher, and Karthika Sasikumar, "Leaders and Laggards: When and Why Do Countries Sign the NPT?," Research Group in International Security, Working Paper 16, November 2004.

Way, Christopher, and Jessica Weeks, "Making It Personal: Regime Type and Nuclear Proliferation," *American Journal of Political Science*, Vol. 58, No. 3, 2014, pp. 705–719.

Weiss, Thomas G., "The United Nations: Before, During and After 1945," *International Affairs*, Vol. 91, No. 6, 2015, pp. 1221–1235.

Wendt, Alexander, "Constructing International Politics," *International Security*, Vol. 20, No. 1, Summer 1995, pp. 71–81.

Werber, Laura, Lawrence M. Hanser, and Constance H. Davis, *The Role of Deployments in Competency Development: Experience from Prince Sultan Air Base and Eskan Village in Saudi Arabia*, Santa Monica, Calif.: RAND Corporation, DB-435-AF, 2004.

Wheelock, David C., "Lessons Learned? Comparing the Federal Reserve's Responses to the Crises of 1929–1933 and 2007–2009," *Federal Reserve Bank of St. Louis Review*, March–April 2010.

White House, "National Security Strategy of the United States," 2015, https://obamawhitehouse.archives.gov/sites/default/files/docs/ 2015_national_security_strategy_2.pdf

———, "Statement by the President on the Trans-Pacific Partnership," October 5, 2015. As of March 14, 2016:
https://www.whitehouse.gov/the-press-office/2015/10/05/
statement-president-trans-pacific-partnership

Wilczyński, Ryszard, and Piotr Graff, "The Role of International Financial Institutions in Poland's Transition to a Market Economy," *Eastern European Economics*, Vol. 32, No. 5, 1994, pp. 36–50. As of January 26, 2017:
http://www.jstor.org/stable/4379975

Williams, David, *The World Bank and Social Transformation in International Politics*, London: Routledge, 2008.

Wilson, Bruce, "Compliance by WTO Members with Adverse WTO Dispute Settlement Rulings: The Record to Date," *Journal of International Economic Law*, Vol. 10, No. 2, June 2007, pp. 397–403.

Wilson, Peter, "The English School Meets the Chicago School: The Case for a Grounded Theory of International Institutions," *International Studies Review*, Vol. 14, 2012, pp. 567–590.

Woods, Ngaire, "The United States and the International Financial Institutions: Power and Influence Within the World Bank and the IMF," in Rosemary Foot, S. Neil MacFarlane, and Michael Mastanduno, eds., *U.S. Hegemony and International Organizations: The United States and Multilateral Institutions*, Oxford: Oxford University Press, 2003, pp. 92–114.

World Bank, "Combatting Corruption," May 11, 2017. As of December 1, 2017:
http://www.worldbank.org/en/topic/governance/brief/anti-corruption

World Justice Project, *Rule of Law Index 2016*, Washington, D.C.: World Justice Project, 2016.

World Trade Organization, *World Trade Report 2007*, Geneva: World Trade Organization, 2007.

Young, Oran R., "Effectiveness of International Environmental Regimes: Existing Knowledge, Cutting-Edge Themes, and Research Strategies," *Proceedings of the National Academy of Sciences*, Vol. 108, No. 50, December 2011, pp. 19853–19860. As of January 12, 2017:
http://www.pnas.org/cgi/doi/10.1073/pnas.1111690108

Zanger, Sabine C., "A Global Analysis of the Effect of Political Regime Changes on Life Integrity Violations, 1977–1993," *Journal of Peace Research*, Vol. 37, No. 2, 2000, pp. 213–233.

Zaring, David, "Network and Treaty Performance during the Financial Crisis," *Proceedings of the Annual Meeting (American Society of International Law)*, Vol. 103, 2009, pp. 63–65.